THE SALES PROCESS UNCOVERED

KEVIN SIDEBOTTOM

THE SALES PROCESS UNCOVERED

A PROVEN PROCESS FOR SALES SUCCESS
AND GAINING INFLUENCE

KEVIN SIDEBOTTOM

The Sales Process Uncovered

ISBN 978-0-578-42151-3

Editor By: Amanda Filippelli
Layout Design: Sarah Beaudin
Cover Design: Amanda Filippelli

Printed in the United States of America

CONTENTS

THE BEGINNING

I have spent over a decade in sales, crafting new ideas about how to reach potential customers. Having worked in multiple industries, selling to end users, small businesses and large corporations, I have been able to validate that this process works, and it works well when applied correctly. This content is not theoretical data, but an actual roadmap that has been developed and applied, refined, applied, and refined more. It has taken extreme amounts of time, strategy, and real-life application of the sales process to achieve results. There have been many iterations along the way, but this finished product has proven time and time again to be very effective and easy to implement. The tactics discussed in this book are very simple to follow, and provide information about the way people react throughout sales transactions and why. It is up to you to choose how you will use this knowledge and apply it.

Salespeople, for the most part, are still thought of today as slimy—as people that only want to make a sale at all costs. Poor sales techniques employed by a small minority of salespeople with the wrong desires in mind have unfortunately cast a dark cloud over the profession. You can either use the information in this book to ethically help people, or use it to manipulate people. The choice is yours, so I ask that you choose wisely. I have chosen to use this information ethically and to serve my clients, and I take pride in doing so.

This book is based upon the principal that sales is a process that can be repeated consistently whether you are selling a product, service, or to get your organization to follow your vision. This also comes as a shock to most people. And with any process, discipline is needed to achieve success. Most of our daily lives consist of a bunch of processes put together to help us move through our day. Some are simple, like tying your shoes, to complex ones, like cooking, which still evades me to this day. Taking any process and repeating it over and over with intentionality will cause it to become a habit, and eventually a behavior that you will not even need to think about as it becomes second nature to you.

Becoming disciplined is not much fun at the start, which is why most people never excel at the skill they set out to learn. Those that are easily influenced to jump from fad to fad will be the ones that are like waves in the ocean, being tossed around by the wind. Use this sales process to help you become a rock star whom others in your organization will want to emulate.

I have always enjoyed helping others get better and move forward. Unfortunately, when I asked other salespeople about how they sell and what steps they go through, most could not define a step-by-step process. Most said, "I don't know. It just happens, I guess." This greatly disturbed me while I was learning sales, so I set out to design a process. Having an engineering mind plus a history of technical schooling, I am a systems implementer by nature. There had to be a process to sales, and I set out to understand it to help others. Let me take you back to help you understand my background and a bit about me.

When I was younger, I never thought I would become a professional salesperson. I was always taught that salespeople are slimy and that you can't trust them. My parents divorced when I was nine years old, and I chose to live with my father, he was a firefighter, but not by choice from what I understand. Before me, he'd attended college to get a degree in dentistry, but unfortunately ran out of money and had to find work. He chose to become a firefighter, like his father and his grandfather. I wanted to be a firefighter, too, like my father, uncle, grandfather and great grandfather. I thought that was a career that would fit me because I like helping people. When I was getting close to high school graduation, my father told me that I should do something more with my life other than being a firefighter. I respected my father's opinion greatly, so I pursued a degree in electrical engineering.

I graduated college with an engineering degree from a well-known university—not a sales or business degree. I had a well-paying career in designing things that most people take for granted, but allow their vehicles move down the road. Something was missing, though, and I could not put my finger on it at the time.

In the fall of 2004, I was at a tailgate with my father, uncle, cousin, and a couple family friends. I was talking to them about the opportunity to take a sales job for a company based in Michigan. My father was furious, screaming that I would be throwing away a degree to be a dumb sales guy—a profession that people call slimy and untrustworthy. But I'm glad that I didn't listen. Since making my journey into sales, I have never looked back, because sales has helped me become a better person than I believe engineering ever could have.

Prior to that difficult discussion with my father, I met with Chris, the owner of a distributorship, who talked to me about giving sales a try. He said that if you want to be a good leader, manage people, or run an organization, then you need to know sales. Sales is the study of people, he said. I was intrigued because I am not someone who just wants to be a gear in a machine, but someone who has purpose, a desire for growth, and again, who helps people.

Chris invested in me to interview with multiple people, had me ride along with some of his top salespeople, had me do personality tests, and also had me give a formal presentation to his vice president and himself as part of the interview process. He had me interview by selling a product line that his company distributes. The scenario was that they were brothers, and Chris played the quiet prick brother that just stared at me to make me uncomfortable. Chris, who can appear intimidating, is a six-foot-five military vet. To say that I was nervous is an understatement. I consider it a pivotal moment that stretched me to become better. To date, I haven't seen or heard about very many companies that will go past a couple interviews for prospective employees. Dave Ramsey shares in his book, *EntreLeadership*, that his company goes one step further and takes their prospective employees and significant others to dinner to really see how the person functions.

After the presentation, Chris met with me and said that I did "okay," and if I was still interested that he would be willing to have me come aboard. During that moment, I came to make the second biggest decision of my life: to change careers. Chris knew business and what it takes to sell, and would imbue me with knowledge about leadership as well as what it really takes in order to succeed. He started his company with an opening revenue of $50,000 and it has grown to nearly $200 million annual revenue, which is exceptional seeing that this business distributes line trimmers, zero turn riders, show removal equipment, two-cycle engines, and the like, so I took his teachings seriously. I took the leap and have not looked back since. I did, however, get some bumps and bruises, especially in the first few years.

As I look back on that decision, though, I am very happy to report that I have made deals that range from hundreds of dollars to multi-million, multi-year contracts. All that I have learned throughout the process has been put into this book to help you, the reader, get better, hopefully without all of the bumps and bruises that I incurred.

This book is to help those of you that want to make an honest living serving your customer. Even if you have never sold before, you can achieve great results from following the process outlined in this book. Even those that have sold before, but who want to get better results, will find the tools to do so. Those that believe they have reached the pinnacle of sales authority can still learn from this book if they humble themselves and understand that no one truly arrives at anything. No matter what skill you have learned, you can constantly improve. This book helps those who want to have consistent success selling while understanding why they sometimes see great results and other times don't. If you want to get the most out of this book, you will need to come with an open mind and to maintain your curiosity about how sales happen.

People are the root of all transactions, and it should also be said that the way people buy is based on relationships. People want to satisfy needs that can range from emotional to basic needs, such as clothing, food, and shelter. It is up to the salesperson to do their best to identify a customer's need, and then find the best product or service that will enable that customer to get where they want to go. The salesperson is also responsible for growing their relationship with a customer in order to obtain the commitments needed from them to get to the next level in their buying decisions, which will be discussed in detail throughout this book.

Putting this sales process to work revealed to me how to generate more sales consistently. I was increasing my sales numbers dramatically, even in the down economy, and was able to apply my process to different industries, resulting in a top salesman award in the United States. The same process can be applied to selling automotive OEMs as it can be used to sell to landscapers. Using the sales process also allows for a salesman to follow up and close more sales by helping the customer achieve in a better, streamlined way. It has been used in business to change customer direction as well as with end users who purchase the product or service. I have also found that if you are, in fact, wanting to lead people, utilizing the sales process allows you to influence others and obtain more buy-in from those around you in order to move forward. The process will work in whatever industry you are in and with whatever demographic you are serving.

I am excited to share my insight on the sales process with you. My hope is that my insight will help those that are just starting out in sales to gain momentum faster, and to help those that have been doing okay to analyze what they are doing well while learning how to capitalize as well as refine their approach. The challenge is to push ego to the side and see the possibility, to fully think through the process whenever you engage a customer, and to work to truly help customers. Doing so will enable you to be very successful and gain lasting relationships with customers, but first, you need to grow, just like I had to.

In the beginning of 2005, I made a change from a comfortable engineer to a sales professional. During the first few months, my mentor, Chris, pulled me aside and said that he wanted me to understand all the operational groups in the company before running out and selling. His reasoning for this was that he knew that anyone can be an average salesperson, but those that really understand how their organization functions can really speak to those areas when in front of the customer. For the first two months, I found myself working in the shipping and receiving department, pulling and packing orders.

In that time, I was able to understand what it really took to process the orders placed by the customers, mostly by fax or phone, and for them to get packed and shipped. Keep in mind, back then, computers were used for processing, not ordering. Websites have come a long way since 2005. It wasn't like now, when anyone can order with a few clicks of the mouse. GPS was still breaking onto the scene, too, so people used these big pieces of paper called maps to get around. I can also tell you that a "thank you" to the personnel who take orders and input them into the system, as well as to the team that packs and ships, is probably overdue by most salespeople. Those are the people that put up with your customers, and your demands, all year, inputting, packaging, and shipping orders. These individuals work very hard. At this point, I should also apologize to a few of my first customers because I probably packaged some of their orders incorrectly during those first couple of months. Shipping and receiving is not a glamorous position, but it is critical to customer satisfaction because this operational team helps customers get the correct parts. In turn, companies acquire repeat customers who are making money with their equipment.

After my time in shipping and receiving, I was to sit down and understand the service team as well as help with their regular trainings. Now, I did not understand all the aspects of every product, but Chris was looking for me to learn how the service team functions. This would help me when talking to mechanics, which were the most important contacts for our customers. I'll dive into that when we talk about selling. I was in service trainings with the dealer mechanics to watch how the organization utilized trainings to help the customer mechanics gain knowledge of the product, best practices for diagnosing issues, and how to properly submit warranty requests for any equipment that may have had experienced a failure that was not caused by misuse. There was a great deal to learn, and even more about how our organization functioned when helping customers with service issues.

Finally, after a few months of inside training, it was my time to hop in the company vehicle and introduce myself to all of the customers. The territory was pretty mature, so it meant that I was to maintain relationships with current business as well as find any potential customers that may have been missed. I loaded up the vehicle with enough literature—brochures and catalogs—to burn down a small forest, if needed. I am talking about boxes upon boxes. A great deal of money is spent on these colorful books of information every year to make sure that people can read up on anything they might desire. It is a relatively old school method, seeing that now you can look everything up online, including videos of products. Still, organizations continued to value paper literature as a way for customers to read up on their product, and I was ready for the maiden voyage!

As I launched out, I quickly found that sales was a great deal more than just numbers. Sales required great strategy, learning the needs of your customer, as well as getting them past the *great-a-new-sales-guy-to-bother-me* mindset. It is about making everyone feel valued and appreciated, not just meeting with the owner or office manager. Everyone from the top down should feel like they are the President of the United States when you meet them.

Also, make sure that the literature racks are fully supplied and cleaned! I didn't figure that literature racks were part of my job description until I had my first tough discussion with Chris during a ride-along. From that day on, guess who made sure that checking literature levels and displays was in my process? I almost skipped saying hello to the customer at the next stop in fear for my life that Chris would miss me checking the literature racks. There's something about an ex-military guy's wording that can help you refocus your priorities.

I pushed hard to sell the products and services that our organization represented, and worked to make great relationships with the customer base. I studied the territory to find out who was doing the majority of business as well as who might be good fits for where we had gaps in our customer base. I performed countless demonstrations with my equipment, went to trade shows to show off equipment, and put in a great deal of driving time in the company vehicle—so much that I swear the seat was shaped to my butt imprint. Sixty to seventy-hour work weeks were the norm for me back then as I wanted to do very well. I worked with other salespeople in our organization to better learn about products and how not to crash them into things when conducting demonstrations.

While I was out on the road for a few weeks, I was sent to a product show in Columbus, Ohio. I am a pretty good driver of anything with a steering wheel, but when I first started selling outdoor power equipment, I quickly learned that the steering joysticks on the equipment were a whole new ball game. I could not make the machine drive straight to save my life. I bounced the machine off of so many things that my coworkers politely asked me to get off the machine and do something less damaging, like assembling displays. They joked about how bad of a driver I was. After that show, I made it a mission to learn how to operate the machines like a professional. I did get my revenge later in my career, though, when I had the opportunity to steer the machines in commercials, driving them up steep inclines and maneuvering the machines like a professional stunt car driver.

The first year of traveling around my territory came to a close, and it was time for my territory review. I had hit a sales record that territory had never seen before... *I sold the equivalent of nothing.* Chris, however, granted me grace during that review and stated it was clear that I would need some help before he was ready to just toss me out. He stated that he would take me under his wing and teach me. I was very grateful for the grace being extended, and I was determined to get better and turn the territory around from there on out! I put my head down and worked hard, studying the products and the competition in great detail. I made spreadsheets on pros and cons for every major product I was competing against, and wanted to know every detail about how the competition worked with their customers.

I also was open to coaching from Chris, which meant that I was going to be meeting him quite often to help after hours and on the weekends with projects. What I didn't know at the time is that I would be getting an MBA in business while I was helping him. He would tell me about business decisions he'd made, why he made them, and what happened as a result. I worked in silence, listening to story after story, the ups and downs, and the reasons for his decisions. While my friends were going to college and learning theory, I was getting the real-life application.

While I think there is benefit to college degrees, I also value real-life application from high performers. I have yet to see a happy middle ground for this, but what I can say is that although I do not have a Master's in business from a college or university, I am often able to show business leaders the *why* and *how* to mitigate risk as well as how they need to approach a situation. Situational awareness has been key in understanding timing and approach, which is a little harder to learn from books. Learning in real time and in real world situations is key. Chris would have me work with him on projects to help get his work done while teaching me.

When I say "projects," I mean clearing an acre of trees for the entire month of August, under brush, making sure nothing was standing except the larger shade trees. I also mean cleaning up older vehicles that were ready to be sold, making deliveries to customers, and projects around the office. These were not the most glamorous of projects, but there were times when I was able to glean an extreme amount of applicable business intellect as well as how to strategize. He shared with me how he judged situations and how he prepared prior to meeting with customers. He also shared some of his bloopers from when he first started out, and what he learned from those improvement opportunities. I got to hear how he managed adversity throughout his start-up and why he kept pushing forward, reinvesting in the organization and himself. I had his undivided attention during this time.

Chris also had multiple trainers come in to train the sales team in various areas. I continue to use the excellent perspectives that I gained in the consulting that I do today. We were learning from sales professionals about sales and identifying the competitive landscape. The trainers used examples from our territory and had us walk through all of the customers and which products were sold to each. They taught on how to quantify a solid prospect, and how to quantify the potential that the prospective customer might have for growth in the market. There were also manufacturer product specialists that came in to train us on the equipment we were selling. The specialists were able to reframe content in a way that we understood, and they taught us how to do the same for the organizations we would be selling to. Chris was right when he said, "Sometimes people need to hear it from someone else before they will believe you." From there, we tried to compete to see who was better. Still being a little new, I was focused on not running anyone over, or cutting an arm off while using a chainsaw.

With all that was invested in me, and from being a sponge, according to Chris, I finally hit my stride and was making sales, landing new customers, and growing my territory a bit. Around the same time, Chris bought a distributorship in Florida. There was an opportunity to grow a smaller product line while the current market was rather low. I walked into the Vice President's office and stated that I was interested in the opportunity to go if a position came up. Oddly enough, there was an opportunity, so off to Florida I went.

I secretly wanted to grow as a person and leave my comfort zone. I wanted to move far away from my family and venture out on my own. I also wanted to see if I had what it took to launch a new territory, and I wanted practice with the sales techniques

I had learned. Within a week, I was on a road trip to Florida to pick up the sales vehicle and a sales manager. We had a full week of meetings with the current customers, and I also had to find a place to live. I settled on Tampa, right in the middle of my new territory—one that would reach from Naples up the West coast, and include the panhandle. I was looking at a lot of windshield time! About 40,000 miles per year actually.

There I was, settled in Florida, and running a territory that was three times larger than my first one. The people there did not know our company, the product very well, or myself. I figured that I could only go up from there. Using what I had learned from sales training and what I remembered from Chris, I put my head down and started running. I was making sales and landing new customers here and there. I was doing okay. Most of what happened in Florida was transactional.

Chris and I had conversations about the territory and how it was coming along. As we talked about the territory and how the customers were responding to the change in the distributorship, he became curious. I shared some of their comments with him, like, "You're a Yankee, aren't you?" meaning they were picking up on my Midwest accent. Chris and I talked about growing trust with the customers and how they could relate to the new organization that was supporting them. That is when Chris decided to send me to Dale Carnegie's training. He had sent other people from our organization to Dale Carnegie's training in the past and he thought it was time for me to take that next step in my development.

This was a weekly training that was really eye opening. The course was called, "Human Relations and Effective Communication." The people in the course were from all different industries, and I think I was one of the few salespeople. During this course, I really came to understand what real relationships are about, how to cultivate great and lasting relationships, and how to help people feel valued. At the end of the day, that is what everyone wants; they want to feel like they have value and are accepted. This course was crucial for me in learning how to build rapport and how to do so very quickly with those I come in contact with.

This course had me jumping around the room, describing stories in front of people I didn't know then, remembering names on the first night (twenty-nine to be exact), and re-learning the Golden Rule: do unto others as you would have them do unto you–something my parents told me all the time as my eyes rolled into the back of my head as a youth. The course taught me how to really engage people on a personal level, and to put such a high value on people that I had no other choice than to want to learn about them and their story. My best memory from the course is of a gentleman named Phil who described a white water rafting trip while sitting on a stability ball, wearing a life jacket and holding an oar. This story was told over ten years ago, and I can remember almost every detail from it and about Phil to this day. The story was so captivating because it made me feel like I was right there with Phil on the trip. It also made me want to book a trip because it sounded very exciting. The course really provided us with con-scious focus about how people hear us when we speak, and how to relate to others in such a way, not to get what we want, but to earnestly help them instead. Putting the focus on others and helping them is not something that most people tend to want to do. We, as humans, are usually focused on what is in it for us and how we can benefit from a transaction as opposed to how we can help the customer through a transaction. I started implementing all that I learned there to help me really understand and relate to my customers on a whole new level.

I didn't know at the time that this was the beginning of the sales process being formed. I often found myself getting so far into a sale, understanding all the issues my potential customer had, but then I wasn't able to make the sale every time. I chalked it up to the fact that sales is a numbers game. When I talked with Chris in a follow-up to see how I was doing, he suggested a few books for me to read that might help. I really did not care to read, but Chris is a very smart person and I respect his opinion, so I started reading those books. After seeing how well I was doing in the beginning of the process, I started drafting some of my past meetings in conjunction with the sales processes that they presented in the books Chris recommended, the Dale Carnegie training, and some of the past trainings I'd had. I was pretty sure I had a solid rough draft for the beginning of the sales process. I called Chris to talk about it and his voice was that of a father watching his kid ride a bike for the first time without training wheels. We talked for quite a while, laughing about some of my bloopers, and I learned how to strategize customer responses and how to maneuver through those objections.

During the discussion, I started thinking about how I could put together all of this data to form one solid process that could be replicated, like tying your shoes. Here is where my engineering mindset came into play. I started to pull together all the data and past meetings with customers to see where and why I failed. I remembered some meetings, like one where I met with a customer that liked my enthusiasm but did not see why my product would work for him. He entertained me and gave me time because I had built a relationship with him, but he just could not consider taking on the product line that I represented. Sitting down and reviewing that conversation revealed that I was not answering his needs, that I truly did not understand his needs or his market. Later, when I did earn his business with that product line, I was able to review *why* and *what* went into his decision to buy from me. It was a constant and grueling review while sitting in hotels, thinking about it during runs on the beach, and while reviewing with Chris. I often asked myself why I got stalled and where I could have done better after each call, and then I'd write it all down in my notes. Development of the process presented in this book took years of review with many customers.

I remember sitting back one night in the hotel, and I could actually visualize the steps in the process, like it was projected on the wall in front of me. I started drafting a diagram on a sheet of paper so that I would not forget it. I started carrying it around with me, and before I entered into a meeting with any customer, I was reviewing my diagram to see where I thought I was in the sales process. I would then review it again when I left the meeting with a customer to see if I was correct about where I was in the sales process. I was "engineering the sales process," as Chris put it one day during a conversation.

This took quite a while for me to understand, and longer to be able to put into words so that others can apply this process as well. I am excited for you to be able to uncover the sales process and increase your effectiveness as well as your sales numbers!

So, let's get started!

YOU, NOT THE PRODUCT

Have you ever met someone and just felt like something was wrong, but you couldn't put your finger on it at that specific moment? Ever met someone that had so much energy, who invaded your personal space, making you feel like pushing them away? Have you ever met someone that you instantly connected with and a friendship sprung from one interaction that has lasted years? How about meeting people who you felt neutral about, meaning if you never saw them again you would not be hurt or happy? We all use buying decision number one when we meet someone. This is the decision that determines whether you like and/or trust someone. This is your customer's first buying decision as well. They are going back and forth in their head, while you are rambling about why they need to know you, and are trying to weigh if you are trustworthy to talk to for more than five minutes.

Potential customers and current customers don't have a lot of time because they are extremely busy with hundreds of events throughout the day. The last thing they have time for while you are prospecting them is to have someone come in and waste their time. Having someone else come in to take up more of their time puts them behind, and they tend to become agitated. It really doesn't matter that you might be bringing the idea that will revolutionize their job forever. Even if you were to hand them a check for a million dollars, some might pass on talking with you... well, maybe they would give you ten minutes for that much.

So, now you finally have five minutes of their time because you spoke about how you can help them. Please remember that you better deliver on that promise to help them. Chris always talked to the sales team about first encounters and asking the target for five minutes even though the conversation would take much longer. That is, if we did our job correctly.

Keep in mind that you may know all of your product specs and be a really nice person, but the customer doesn't know that. Sales, just like leadership, is based on influence. If you cannot influence your customer and others around you, it will be a hard-fought battle trying to gain their trust. Trust is the only collateral when trying to gain influence. Every step builds upon the previous step, so keep that in mind when you are working through the sales process. You better make sure you have sold yourself as the expert as well as shown them that you can be trusted. References from other customers similar to the one you are interacting with is a great way to help build trust, especially if they know the reference on a personal level.

Be genuine and authentic with those that you interact with. Be yourself, and don't try to only sell the best version of you. People will learn about all of your traits in the end. You don't want to give them all the bad things about you, but let people in and let them learn why you do what you do. Let them learn why you are there to help them and why you are a decent person that they will be able to trust. Remember: a fake is easily sniffed out.

Remember that you only have a short amount of time to get a customer engaged and curious about what you are talking about, it is wise to make sure you are hitting them with the fact that you are trustworthy and that you can offer them value. Customers also want to feel like they are buying a product or service, and not being sold something. People don't like to feel like they were not a part of the discussion, and that the salesperson was just selling the product without getting to know if the product actually meets their needs. Some people will just buy things from pushy salespeople just so the salesperson will leave them alone. It's crazy that it happens, but usually, within a few days, the person returns the product.

After a person is sold something is when buyer's remorse sets in, following the transaction. Buyer's remorse degrades the trust that the customer has for the salesperson. When people buy, they have a sense of accomplishment in finding something that meets their needs, and in the belief that this product or service will help them. Make sure that you have given value and enough of a reason that they have no choice but to keep progressing with you, or schedule a follow-up appointment to really go deeper.

So, you better ask yourself, why should they want to follow up with me?

People buy for many reasons, and as a salesperson, your job is to understand that reason and help the customer navigate that process. Sometimes that means helping the customer buy from your competitors if your product is not right for them. Blow your customer's mind next time you are talking with them and show them a product that might benefit them instead of selling your product.

Now, I am not suggesting always selling other people's products, but if that product actually does help them and better fits their needs, help them.

You will greatly gain a potential customer's trust by fulfilling their needs. I know you are probably thinking in your head that I am crazy: "Is he really telling me to sell someone else's product instead of mine?" The answer is maybe and no. I am pushing you to build trust and use honesty with the customer. Play the long game, and not the short game. Don't be one of those telemarketers selling extended vehicle warranties. They are annoying!

Everyone loves talking about themselves, which is hard when you are a salesperson because your job is mostly listening to the customer to find where you can help them. Focus on bringing great value to them, and listen to them as they will tell you where they need help. Know their industry well so that you can effectively help them. This can include knowing all sorts of facts and figures that might help them be more efficient and gain a competitive advantage.

You might be asking right about now, *Where can I get that information?* I'm sure your organization has some intelligence on the market, like how much of a certain product is sold, who is selling it, which is the most popular product in a set, etc. You should also be doing your homework to understand the market as well. Research by asking end users, do internet searches, surveys (not necessarily standing in a mall with a clipboard—you can just simply ask people in conversation). I used to stalk landscapers to learn where they bought, why they bought the brands they used, what they liked, and what they did not like. I got my information from doing demonstrations of my products, asking the crews after I passed out waters to them, and when I was at gas stations around lunch time.

I make cold calls in new territories all the time while riding with people or selling myself. I study the person that I will be engaging to learn about them. Some might call it stalking, but I call it intelligence gathering. I want to learn about my potential customer so that I can build rapport. When I do ask for a commitment to engage them, I want them to feel comfortable and not like I am just focused on selling, but on helping them. There are many sites out there where you can find information on people: LinkedIn,

Facebook, Twitter, Instagram, Google searches, etc.

If I am entering a customer's location of business and cannot find any information about them prior, I tend to use the Columbo approach. If you weren't around in the seventies and eighties, you might need to look up the show. I passively wander around the area until the curious potential buyer walks up and asks me what I am doing there. Sometimes, if I am able to, I walk in through the service area and gather knowledge from the working department of the company. I see if I can find any opportunities for improvement there. At one of the "Big Three" automotive OEMs, I would ask around to find out who the engineers are for a specific commodity.

In the first few minutes of talking with customers and their team, I offer information to help them with the commitment of giving me only a few minutes of their time. Be aware that their time is important to them as they are most likely putting out fires that have arisen throughout the day. They do not have tons of time for someone to come sell to them. Being aware, I share insight about what we've gone over in the past few minutes. I ask if they want me to continue sharing and having a discussion, or if I should come back at a better time for them.

At that point, they either say that they have some more time and we can carry on with the conversation, or they ask to schedule a date. We lock it in no more than a week out. I want to keep the information fresh in their minds. I pull out the calendar and book the next time and get them to commit. Typically, when you state you have intelligence to share with the potential customer, they are more than willing to have you either keep talking or come back. People like to receive and be helped. They also tend to be reciprocal because they want to help others when they are helped. Subconsciously, when someone helps you, your brain instantly wants to find a way to help them to even up. Call it primal instinct or whatever you want, but it is true.

After obtaining the commitment to keep going, or for the follow-up, I maximize my time by reviewing the customer's office, the products they sell, the engineer's cube, the manager's office, etc. I begin to build rapport with them by finding common ground as well.

In the lawn industry, I found that the best salespeople for dealers are actually the lawn dealer mechanics. The reason for this is because they learn what is wrong with certain machines and give honest feedback to the landscapers. Landscapers trust the mechanics so much that they make financial decisions based on their recommendations. Talking to the mechanics about the company, seeing they were used to giving honest feedback, spilled out all the details. They told me who made the decisions. I always make it a point to talk with the mechanics and thank them for their hard work and time. Making sure mechanics are happy is a great way to learn all the areas to exploit against your competitors.

Another area of expertise is demography. Demographers are professionals that study people and how they act. Since sales is the study of people and demographers also study people, it only makes sense that one compliments the other. Demographers study the tendencies of segments of people. They can be hired to do studies for you as well as for your specific market. Knowledge is key, so do your research and know your market. This will also be a constant learning process as markets do evolve with time, so stay on the path of learning.

One thing I also pride myself on is that I never want to be the lowest price. I want to be the salesperson with the most value that can help the customer. I often hear salespeople say things like, "Everyone just wants the cheapest price." I truly do not believe that unless the competing products are exactly identical. Then the only differentiator is price. If a customer sees a specific value in something, they will pay more for it than a competing brand that may be similar. I often share the proverb that my grandfather gave to me: you get what you pay for. When was the last time you bought a discounted item that was similar to the product you wanted and found out later that there was a reason for the discount?

This is a reason why Mercedes, Delta Airlines, and Apple sell a great deal of product at a higher price than most of their competition and with higher profit margins. Each example requires higher prices on their product, but also a great deal more benefits than their lower cost competitors. This is not to say that the competition is horrible and that you should never use the competition. That choice is totally up to you. What I am saying is that these examples offer great value, but also have higher price tags.

In the early days of the iPhone, Apple revolutionized the cell phone and people lined up for days to be the first to obtain one of these amazing pieces of technology, while the competitors struggled to obtain some market share with inferior products. People spend more money on a Mercedes sedan compared to a Hyundai because of the higher quality standards that are in place, such as better leather, ride quality, and technology inside of the vehicles. Delta usually offers flight changes without a need for fees, unlike some of the competitors. You also get a free carry-on bag. You are not nickled and dimed for trip extras like on Spirit airlines. Spirit airlines is also a great example of what seems to be a lower cost, only to find out that when you add all of the extras, you pay the same price, if not more, than Delta.

I work hard to bring value and show that I am an advocate for the customer. This pays dividends when I am working deals with them as well as others in their organization. When I help my customers get to where they want to go, they, in turn, want to help me with something. I don't do this so that they feel obligated to pay me back in the future, but there is something to be said for referrals. A referral from a customer can help you to meet other similar organizations, especially if your customer is a well-respected organization. Referrals speak louder than any marketing ad I have ever seen. People want to trust who they are dealing with and when they are introduced to an organization or product from their respected colleagues, trust is created quickly. Make sure you are looking at your best customers that you deal with today to see if they would be willing to give you a referral or two.

If you are new to an organization and receive a request for quotation from a customer, don't simply answer with numbers like everyone else. Really understand the request, and if there is anything that is missing that would benefit them greatly. For instance, if they request a quote on a product or service but their parameters are off, engage them about why you will not be able to quote them due to the fact that some of their data is off. Showing you are an expert and can help them will interest them in the fact that they may have missed something. Offer to meet with them to discuss how their parameters may be changed to improve their request. Help the customer become better for free. Information is key to leveraging relationships. Helping them will also build credibility, showing them that you are, in fact, an authority.

Keep in mind that people want to have a great buying experience. There is also so much invested in making the process easy. Look at Amazon one-click, and Apple, where you can literally use your Apple app to buy something in their store. They actually hide the cash registers at Apple in hopes you will use the app, because people are likely to buy more using credit cards than cash. Amazon's one-click buying is valuable because who has time for two clicks? I mean, really. Making it easier to buy from you is highly valuable, and being polite and easy to deal with is huge!

SALES PROCESS, STEP 1:

OVERALL OBJECTIVE

The first step is actually a step that will continue until the customer takes action and you sell the product. This step also runs the duration of the sales process and sometimes changes as the outcomes of each step evolve the process. What you first set out to do will be modified if questions arise later in the process, opening other possibilities to help your customer.

Step one is called "Overall Objective." It is the first step mainly because you need to understand what you are trying to accomplish as a professional salesperson. What is your overall goal for the potential customer? Keep in mind that the scope you originally set out with might change as you work through the sales process. During discussions, you may uncover some things that can help you gain more business with your customer as you sell your other services, or it may change because they are in the process of being bought out by one of your current customers. These are a just a couple of examples, but keep in mind that the scope of the overall objective will take different shapes as you work through the process, especially when dealing with multiple decision makers.

You may walk in thinking that you want them to buy one of your top products, but find out that you could help them with multiple items as well as a revolutionary partner system that your organization offers. Do some planning about what your overall objective is. There is a quote attributed to Abraham Lincoln that states: "Give me six hours to chop down a tree and I will spend the first four sharpening the axe." This means you will become more efficient if you plan first and execute second. You wouldn't shoot a gun before checking down range and looking through your sight, would you?

Having a plan means that you need to sit down and review what will be shared, what will be asked, and what benefits you will offer to the customer. One thing my early mentor in sales shared with me to help me focus on the meetings I held with customers was to think about having to hand the customer a bill after your interaction for $500. This was odd to me because I never really thought of my role as charging the customer for the interaction, but if you really think about it, there is something to gain from this mental picture. If I did not prepare well and asked my customer to pay, they might say no.

If you are going to have a meeting with someone, make sure you have a plan in place, and know the purpose for the meeting. Make sure that you have provided enough value to the customer that they would be willing to pay a bill to you for the interaction. Make sure you have strategized effectively and don't just show up. Time wasters will not be asked to come back again and this is your chance to make a great impression. Plan ahead and be prepared to add value.

COMMITMENTS THROUGHOUT THE SALES PROCESS

Throughout the entire sales process, you will be asking for commitments. These commitments are needed in order to get your customer to move forward with you through the sales process together. They will also help you gauge where you are at in the sales process. If there is no commitment from both parties then there is no movement in any process. Stay focused on your overall objective and where you are at in the sales process when asking for the commitments so that you can work together with the customer and help them.

As the salesperson, you want to be very easy to deal with, have a plan, and be willing to earn small commitments from the customer throughout the sales process. It is almost like a bunch of small sales on your way to the big overall objective you set out to reach. The first commitment that you are working towards is the commitment of time. The amount of time you are trying to get the customer to commit to should be equal to how much value you bring to them. With that being said, a quick five to fifteen minutes should be sufficient to leave them with a bit of value and a desire to continue to the next meeting where you can discuss more details.

I will align the commitments with the phase of the selling process in order to keep it easy to follow as we move through each phase. I will also include the commitment at the beginning of each selling step for consistency. Commitments are different for different kinds of organizations you will encounter as well. I am typically someone that looks at the big picture, but I have learned that owner-operators and end users tend to be the decision makers, or may have one other decision maker, especially if they are married. Larger organizations have moved to a collaborative approach, which means not one person makes a decision mainly because no one wants to be the guy that gets blamed if something goes wrong. I say that with a bit of humor, but there is still a little truth to it.

The commitments will look a little different at times, but sometimes the same commitment follows both organizational types. The first meeting is typically the same for all scenarios, which is time. You need someone to really champion, and getting them on board is easier than trying to sell to a group of people.

Have you ever stopped to think about those people that call your cell phone to sell to you, even though you are on the Do Not Call list? I have to work to not get angry when the salesperson for extended car warranties calls my phone. I keep telling myself to give them a chance. One guy who called me had such a great approach that I just had to stay on the phone and let him keep going, even though I still do not own the 2013 Jeep Wrangler they insist I have. He was so good at building rapport that I stayed on the call until he passed me on to his supervisor. That is when the call went downhill, and fast. The supervisor even tried to close me while I said I no longer owned the vehicle. This supervisor was very pushy to the point I said, "STOP," and asked him if he wanted to make the sale. He, of course, said yes. I then told him to talk to the guy that transferred me to him so that he could really understand how to sell, because what the supervisor was doing was only going to piss people off. Don't be that supervisor that chases away potential customers with hard closing techniques that went out with the eighties.

The first gentleman that called me was great and got me to commit to talking to the next guy. He earned my commitment by being personal and polite, which is lost by most salespeople today.

SALES PROCESS, STEP 2:

RAPPORT

Step two is "Rapport." I tend to pride myself on being able to build rapport quickly when meeting people face-to-face due to my extensive training, being able to take the temperature of the room, and the ability to help people relax. A great deal of years and money has been spent for me to be able to make that statement, though. Being intentional about how the situation unfolds is important for you to be able to start the process of building rapport with people. They will be on their guard the moment they meet you if they do not know you. Plan how you will introduce yourself, which colors you will wear, and research the person you are meeting.

During this step, you are working to get a commitment from the customer that requires their time. This commitment should not require extensive amounts of time for interaction with the customer. By being polite and respecting their time, they will be more likely to ask you to come back for a more in-depth conversation at a later date. Be ready to schedule that next interaction with them. Below is a quick reference for the commitment that you will be asking for in the rapport step.

Commitment
Owner-Operator/End User = Time
Multiple Decision Makers = Time

When working the rapport step of the sales process, you must keep in mind that the commitment you are asking for is equal to the value you are going to bring to the customer. This step is a lot like gaining influence in that you need to show value for others to want to hear you and follow you. In this step, time is again the commitment you need from the customer, which means you have to equal that time commitment with the value you are bringing. The value should be in the knowledge you can offer about their environment as well as knowledge of some topic that you might know about that they've expressed interest in.

Obtaining this commitment of time allows you to start the process of building rapport so they can see that you are someone that will bring value to them. This is usually enough to get small pockets of time. I would not ask for hours upon hours of their time. Remember, they are fighting fires, and you don't have the rapport or relational collateral to be asking for large portions of their time. You will have enough time to share some details of the environment they are in that shows you are an expert that can help them. When they see that you have value to offer, they will see a benefit in engaging with you and giving you more time.

I spend time online looking up prospects and learning about them from a business standpoint, but when it comes to their personal side, that research is usually done when you meet them in person. When you have a prospect, client or customer, you should always be trying to learn about them. What are their hobbies, family dynamics, goals in business, aspirations, etc.? When they think of something, even if it is not in the products that you sell, they should be thinking about how you will be someone that can help them. Rapport is like influence in that the more you have, the better suited you are to engage people. Having references that know your potential customer will help you to learn about them and give you common ground to bring up in conversation with them, helping to build rapport.

One process that I have incorporated into my routine when meeting new people is that I use the mental picture of walking up to a nice brick house with a chimney, green yard, white picket fence, and a mailbox. As you walk up, you see the name on the mailbox. As you enter into the yard, you notice toys scattered around, a dog house, and how well the yard is kept up. You start thinking to yourself, *Do they have kids, pets, are they seriously OCD about their yard care?* As you knock on the door and peek through, you see the kids playing, and while waiting outside for someone to answer, you notice an airplane on top of the chimney. You are learning how many kids there are, their ages, and what hobbies they like.

When I am talking with customers, I am looking around the room for pictures, trophies, interests outside of their daily grind at the office. I am intentional about learning about them and what they value. What organizations do they associate with, who are their friends, and what do they like? People really want to have engagement with others, but only if they find common ground. Use these other people that you might know as referrals. If they know this customer and they really like you, why not ask them to offer help? Are there associations that they are involved in that you can help you connect the dots? LinkedIn also helps you see who they know that you know. Having a friend introduce you to the prospect is better than cold calling, hands down.

Building rapport is also a constant act. You want to continually learn more information from the customer and the others they work with. As you start becoming someone they view as a trusted consultant, you will uncover opportunity after opportunity to influence and help them. My focus is on helping my customers not only with the product that I sell but where I can offer help in any aspect of their business. If I can make their lives better with my knowledge then I am improving their lives. You can do that while you are presenting your information that they agreed to listen to on how to help their business. While doing so, season in some questions about their family, who they are, what their passions are, etc. to build some rapport.

For rapport to be worth anything, a solid value needs to be placed on the customer. You really want to know someone that you are working to partner with. It's just like when you are dating someone. As you start a relationship, you continually learn about them as you want to develop the relationship; constantly trying to learn something new about the person. As an added bonus of building rapport with people, you can find out their values. If their values do not line up with yours, you can learn that now so you don't make the mistake of entering into a venture with someone that will be a great deal of stress to work with. This is both a business lesson and a personal life lesson. Make sure you vet potential customers well.

If you do not vet customers correctly, it can cause you a great deal of difficulty in the future. I had one customer that kept asking me to sell them my product and that they would respect territories, but I had a feeling that something was not right. When I talked to other customers as well as my competitors in the area, asking them about this organization, I heard the same thing from everyone about their lack of values, that they weren't paying their bills, and making the lives of salespeople very difficult. This customer was well known for their lack of values, and I can say that making the decision to not sell to them was the best decision for my territory. I was slandered by this dealer, but told by other customers that they respected me more for not setting up that organization. This paid off as my current customers sold more in that territory as a result.

Too often, salespeople just want to be superficial so that they can talk about their product, which might be anything from lawnmowers to dental equipment to the electrical architecture of an automobile. The problem is that you need rapport to be able to come back and build your influence. If you jump right into how great you and your product are, it makes people feel like you don't really care about them and they shut off their attention, counting the seconds until you leave. To win, it is vital to really put value on others above yourself.

There are many other areas that help you build rapport with customers that, if you don't pay attention to, you could miss out on. What color you wear to a meeting can be a trigger for the customer and unconsciously raise their agitation level. Studies show that different colors are associated with different things. I tend to wear light blue and white when meeting someone for the first time. It presents trustworthiness and calmness, whereas red tends to mean "stop," hence traffic lights and stop signs. Tone and pitch can also raise agitation levels. A fast-talking northerner talking to people in Florida tends to drive them insane. Want to know how I know that? I used to get comments like, "You're a Yankee," to which I would reply with, "No, I'm a Detroit Tigers fan," and they would laugh, which broke the tension. Laughter is a great way to break down walls.

Another thing to be aware of when building rapport is how people like to be engaged through their personality traits. There are a great deal of personality assessments and trainings to help you identify personality traits as well as learn how to talk to these traits. Every assessment uses something to categorize people, such as colors, letters, animals, etc. There are more in-depth analysis programs to really understand how each person engages, but for the purposes of this book, I will focus on the DISC method as it is well known, easy to use, and the one that I prefer.

In the DISC method for understanding people, a D (Dominance) person wants straight-to-the-point information and how it will impact them, whereas a C (Compliance) person wants tons of details, and fears making a wrong decision. They are very cautious and want to be very accurate before making a decision. The I (Influence) person is the life of the party, full of enthusiasm, is friendly, optimistic, and looking for the next party to lead everyone to. The S (Steadiness) person is sincere, patient, and very modest. They tend to take the most time to make a decision, and if you are a high D, an S person will drive you crazy.

It is good to understand the different personality types, but I don't believe you must have a Master's degree in them to be successful. Being intentional with your customer and understanding their personality will help you. You may have all the information in the world and be the greatest salesperson, but if you trigger something that generates a negative effect then you aren't going anywhere in the process.

I was always taught that a salesman needs to have the knowledge to identify the DISC profile of the person they are speaking with. Again, I don't believe you need to be able to dissect the person's personality in depth before you can sell to them. Rather than trying to analyze the buyer to discover their hidden DISC metric, I believe there is an easier way to break down buyers that comes out in their behaviors, even more quickly when they answer questions.

In my experience, there are three types of buyers. Each is equally important, especially when selling to a corporation where decisions are made in collaboration with each department. The first type of buyers are the specialists who are more interested in specifications and how the product or company meets technical and identified needs. They are very detail oriented and can be very technical, like engineers and department managers. How successful they are at using what you are selling will directly affect them in their career advancement goals. These people will want to know all the gritty details and will be able to tell if you are not familiar with your product. They may even call you out on it.

The second kind of buyers are the users. The user-buyers are those that will be operating the product. They are usually dental hygienists, nurses, and mechanics. These are the people that are really key to engage as they are the ones using the products all the time. They are the most important people to engage to understand how the competition is doing. They can tell you what they like and don't like in application. Keep them in mind when working through the selling process. These are the people that you want to build a relationship with so that you can ask them how they would design the product to improve it for your research and development team. They tend not to be into all the specifications of a product, but care more about how it works while they are using it.

To give you an idea of the difference between the specialists and the users, think of an engineer and a mechanic. Engineers design fantastic vehicles with big engines that fit tightly into the engine compartment. The mechanics are the ones who have to fix the problems, and figure out ways to work on the engine in such a tight configuration. A lot of times, you will see the mechanic welding up items so they can get into the bends and tight areas to make their life easier.

The third kind of buyer is the final decision maker. They are impacted by the return on their investment. The decision maker takes a 10,000 foot view of everything, and wants to make sure they are profitable. The main decision maker will ask for input from the other two buyers before they make their final decision. This buyer is the last person to focus on as the other two buyers will have the main decision maker's trust. This is the case for most organizations today. The final decision maker will likely be hard for you to make contact with, so you have to work through the others until they are sold on the product and willing to let you speak to the decision maker. The final decision makers want to know what their return will be on the investment, and they want to understand how much time it will take for them to become profitable. They will ask the other two buyers for assistance, and be willing to make the decision fast. Be ready to present when you have this chance as you will not have a second chance to make a first impression.

For owner-operators and end users, they will likely fall into all three of these buyer styles as they need to. Some people are very technically oriented and use the product themselves day-in and day-out. They are also the final decision maker that is thinking about how this investment will impact them. How will they make money on this purchase and how soon will they see success? These will be their main questions when entertaining your presence.

For any organization, asking the best questions to uncover needs is crucial for you to be successful. Below is a graphic of the three types of buyers and how to identify them.

	Specialist	User	Final Decision Maker
How To Identify	Meets Target Goals	Makes My Life Easier	10,000 ft view of decisions
Who They Are	Engineer, Office Manager	Mechanic, Dental Hygienist	CEO, Owner, General Manager
Their Interests	Meets Specifications	Performance / Ease of Use	Return On Investment
What Success Looks Like	Career Advancement if successful	Increased Efficiency / making more money	Increased Productivity / Profits

While you are meeting with any of the types of buyers, I recommend asking for permission to take notes about what you talk about. Usually, they will be flattered that someone is really taking an interest in them. It also shows that you are humble and that you are very interested in them. Think about if someone were to break out a pad of paper and write down notes on what they talked to you about. How would you feel? Chances are you would think that you can trust them a little more than someone that jumps right into how great they are and how their product is going to help you solve world hunger. This will also help you remember details that would otherwise be lost.

Being that we can't remember everything about people, I recommend making a customer profile sheet or use a customer relationship management system (CRM). When you get back into your vehicle, write down what you learned so that you can review before the next time you are in front of the person. If you do not currently have a CRM system that you can enter the data in, I have added a visual of an account profile that I have used for years in multiple industries in the appendix of this book. I have also blogged about meeting minute formats.

Once you have built rapport with the customer, and they are talking to you about their business and what they view as the direction they want to go, you can begin really pulling information out of them. This is where you are about to find out how you can help them to get to a better way. They will also be receptive to you asking more in-depth questions about their organization, values, pain points, future dreams, etc. These are areas that you want to focus on in the next step of the sales process to pull out information as they start telling you things in confidence. Once that rapport is there, customers will confide in you and ask for your suggestions on how to help.

Please do not jump into your sales pitch just yet. You have good amount of work to do, but feel very confident that you are on the right track if they are giving you information. When I say "information," I mean answers that are longer than *yes* and *no*. The customer is actually telling you personal information, and how that information affects them and their business. Once you are here, you are entering into the next step in the sales process. The tension is also very low compared to when you first talked to your potential customer, and you are on your way to pulling the information you need to build your sales presentation.

Congrats! It is time to enter the third step in the sales process!

SALES PROCESS, STEP 3:

UNCOVERING NEEDS

While you work through building rapport with the customer, please keep in mind that you only asked for a few minutes. Sometimes the customer is engaged enough to want to keep going. If so, you are doing an awesome job at building rapport. Leverage as much as you can to uncover their needs. This can be done during the meeting when you are building rapport, and I strongly emphasize doing so, but also can be a separate meeting that you schedule to follow-up with and which includes a more in-depth analysis with them.

You will need the commitment of trust from the customer. They have to trust you a bit to share details about their organization with you. Without the trust component, you are not going to be able to move forward in the sales process or their buying decisions. Below is a quick reference for the commitment that you will be asking for in step three.

Commitment
Owner-Operator/End User = Trust
Multiple Decision Makers = Trust

The "Uncover Needs" step is the most crucial step in the sales process. If you do not work this step correctly, you will have issues later in the process and end up circling back to this step. Take your time to make sure you understand this step before moving on to other steps. I also recommend breaking out a pad of paper and a pen for this step as I walk you through. This was the hardest step for me to solidify while uncovering the sales process and putting it to use.

Uncovering needs is a process of asking questions that pull information out of the person that you are having a conversation with. Unfortunately, most salespeople don't ask enough questions and go straight for the shotgun approach to selling. The salesperson will start rattling off all the features of their product in hopes that the customer will jump out of their seat and hug the salesperson, thanking them for opening up their eyes to this amazing product. Unless your product is the one that ends cancer forever without harming anything else in the body, I say stop, please, stop doing this. Yes, I was guilty of doing this until one customer said, "Those are great. How do they help me?" and stopped me in my tracks. So, please, start asking questions before rattling off awesome details.

When I first started in sales, I was talking with a landscaper in Chicago during a landscape show. I had memorized all the literature and knew the benefits of my product like the back of my hand. When the unsuspecting victim of my awful sales pitch showed up, I was ready to wow them. I told them all the great things about the lawnmower that I was showing them and, in mid-sentence, the landscaper said, "Stop. Can you talk to me about the spindles?"

I said, "Sure!" and was off to the front of the machine to show them what a spindle was on the front wheel. I grew up around cars, so I instinctively knew that the front wheel of a car is held on by a spindle. The spindle on a lawnmower is actually what the cutting blade is attached to. So while we were looking at the front wheel of the lawnmower, the landscaper said, "I meant the deck spindle."

He educated me about what a deck spindle is and how he did not like the design of my lawnmower. He also commented about other features that I had spouted off. He said they were great and might help others, but asked, "How do they, in fact, help me?"

I quickly walked the landscaper over to another salesperson and told him that gentleman might be able to help him better. I then listened in on the other salesperson. He started asking the landscaper questions, and I watched how the same features that I spoke of were later translated into benefits that the landscaper agreed would help him. Life lesson learned. Listen more, talk less, and take a lot of notes!

There are all types of questions, from open to close-ended questions, leading questions, personal questions, etc. You have to earn the right to ask the last one, usually after you have built up a relationship with the person that you are engaging. An open-ended question is one that allows the person responding to state something that can be used to go more in-depth on the topic. For example, you might ask someone, "What is the largest factor that would allow you to see yourself as a success in your current position?" A close-ended question is something that the person can respond to with yes or no. I tend to try and stick with open-ended questions, but let it flow if closed-ended questions come up. The personal questions should come when you begin uncovering needs so you can ask how their needs affects them as an individual. Answers to personal questions will help you map out different types of buyers, as discussed in the previous chapter.

I was told when I started in sales to always ask open-ended questions. What I found is that it is hard to come up with all open-ended questions, and people tend to start getting defensive when you keep prying more and more into their lives. I once had a business owner say that I really asked some in-depth questions that were making him feel uncomfortable, and that our discussion was getting close to ending because of it. I quickly reaffirmed him that I was only asking so as to understand him as best I could. Then I threw in a few close-ended questions until he felt more relaxed. That is why I tend to mix it up a bit and add a little humor to lighten up the mood. I let the conversation flow mainly out of curiosity about the person. I am curious how people view their business and what they view as success, but I also get to know them as a person. People tend to give up more information when they feel you are like them. Pay attention to their posture as well during the conversation and mirror it if you can to allow them to feel more comfortable with you.

While asking these questions about who they are as individuals, why they are in business, and what their values are, also be focused on asking questions that will highlight the benefits of what you are selling them. Learn as much as you can from the customer while you have undivided attention with them. Learn who the decision makers are, what their greatest needs are, what will make them feel successful, and you can sprinkle in some questions about who their greatest competitor is. You should know the answer as you have studied the market, but you may be surprised to find out who they believe it to be. They may even be right. Remember, you are learning as much as you can about them. Later, you will see how to structure questions to effectively bring to light the features and benefits of your product.

Asking questions, such as about time frames for when they might want to implement a change, will help you understand how much faster you need to work, or if they are not ready yet, you know to keep them in mind. Far too often, salespeople say they have a "hot lead" or "prospect," but if they would have identified when the customer might want to make a change, they would be able to focus energy in another area. The salesperson often forgets to follow up, and the next person in line gets the deal. Don't leave that opening for the competition.

Finding out who all is involved will help you garner some understanding of the organization and who the main decision maker is. The main decision maker may be out of the office on a golf trip with your competitor. Wouldn't that be of value to know—that he likes to golf and that your competitor is ahead of you?

So, how can you structure questions that highlight your product? How do you structure questions that you can ask customers that highlight the benefits of what you're offering? This process involves tying back benefits to form questions. The stronger the question, the better the benefit is highlighted when it is uncovered.

I'll use a graphic to illustrate this process of creating questions to pull out benefits from your product or service's features:

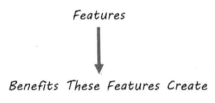

Take out a sheet of paper and a pen and start listing features of your product. List the features across the top of the sheet of paper from left to right, making each feature into a column. Below each feature, list a benefit that each feature creates. For example, when doing trainings with slides, I use my clicker that has a little button that makes the slide I am on go black. The feature is the button that I can push to make the slide go blank. The benefit is that I can then draw attention back to me and keep people from trying to read ahead on the slide. Feature = button, benefit = gaining attention.

Below the benefit, write down the needs that the benefit answers. The graphic is extended into the next step of the question creating process.

Using the same example, the magical button that makes the screen go blank and offers me the benefit of gaining attention, ask: what need is answered by the benefit? For me, I use the fact that I need to draw back the attention of the audience to expand on a point I am trying to make. I may also want to share a personal story of how I screwed up something in the past so they don't do the same in the future. The need that is being answered is refocusing attention.

Need
Answered

Questions to Pull Out Need

Now we have to figure out the question that we can ask that both answers the need and highlights the benefit that the feature addresses. List below the needs answered, in the same column, a few questions that you could ask. Here are a couple I would use: Would it be beneficial if you had a way during your presentation to refocus the group back to you so that you could enhance the point you want to get across? How much greater influence do you think you would have when training people if you could pause the presentation to highlight a point that needs to be addressed in more detail?

Below is the complete process of creating the questions that tie back your features and benefits:

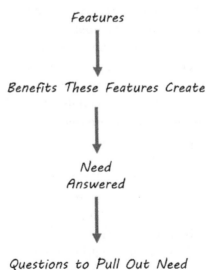

Features

Benefits These Features Create

Need
Answered

Questions to Pull Out Need

When I used to sell stand-on riding lawnmowers that held inclines and fit in tighter areas than traditional lawnmowers, I would ask questions about whether the customer had ever had any employees trapped upside down when a mower flipped over, had read about some of these incidents, or about the areas they had to maneuver around. I would follow up with questions about how they currently handle those areas, and so on and so forth. I was aligning them with the fact that my product could move around, and if the operator got into a bad spot, they could simply step off the back and be safe.

I tried to pull out as much information on current issues, and if I could help them, then the customer viewed it as a win for themselves. When people feel the emotional impact of where they are and where they want to go, they become more open and trust you. I used this practice in the automotive industry while talking to engineers as well. It works there even better because engineers will tell you all the issues with your competition if you let them!

I had to use questions to help out a customer of one of the larger organizations in my territory. When dealing with engineers on an architecture project, and your organization owns the patent on software that can do calculations for the engineers in minutes, when it would take them days or weeks, one might ask, "If the software can run the calculations in minutes, what else would the engineer be able to accomplish?" Seeing that engineers value efficiency, they would answer very positively to this.

Maybe this might allow them to focus on moving modules around in a vehicle faster, saving the automotive organization $8–$12 per vehicle. In the automotive industry, they sell roughly 500,000 trucks annually, which equates to millions of dollars. So money is important, but much more than that, the company can now sit with other platforms and really help design an efficient vehicle when there are so many constraints. Vehicles are getting smaller, but technology requests in vehicles keep increasing. The fight for space is huge in the automotive world. Teams argue about which modules take precedence. So, helping all the teams work together and understand the big picture of how all the modules can fit together is valuable. It also allows them to save millions; not that the end user would see that savings unless they own stock in the company.

To further understand the focus of questions during the sales process, let's look at how your questions might mirror what Simon Sinek refers to as the "Golden Circle." Simon is widely known for his TED Talk on the "Golden Circle." He focuses in on how ultra-successful organizations don't focus on what they sell. They go past the "how" and straight to "why" they are in business. He uses Apple as one of his examples of an ultra-successful company that focuses on why they exist. Keep this in mind when you are creating your questions. Below is an example of the "what, how, why" reframed.

Simon's Golden Circle   Needs Bullseye

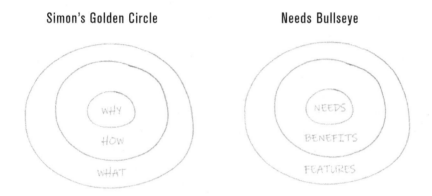

The key is to make your features and benefits flow from the why and tie right back into how they really improve your customer's life. You should also figure out questions that will highlight benefits from your organization that you represent. Why does your organization exist? How do your features and benefits answer the "why" of your organization? This is a tough objective, but if you want people lining up for six hours for your product like Apple does, it is totally worth the effort. So, I challenge you to study Apple, Google, and all those other companies that seem to have most of the market share compared to others in the same arena.

If you do your homework and really strive to help your customer to a better way as well as communicate it to them effectively, they will see you as the authority. Knowing their company, though, is the hard part. Do your research on your customer's company and on the customer as an individual as well.

With trial and error, you will learn which questions work well and how to revise them to make them even better. Repeat the process to improve, because no one gets it right on the first try. You can do it. You have all the answers, now you just need to learn the right questions to ask.

I hate role playing, but it has been proven in studies that it works effectively. Think of the Navy Seals. They work so efficiently to win each battle they face, and it's because they actually role play each scenario over and over again until it is second nature to them.

Another great tactic that has helped me when drawing out information is the mirroring tactic. This tactic is used by hostage negotiators in order to obtain information from suspects on the other end of the phone. The hostage negotiator has to identify all aspects of the scenario, not just what the suspect wants. They have to find ways to get hostages out safely. One way they do this is to mirror the last three words the suspect says in order to draw out more information.

Mirroring makes the unconscious mind want to explain more in depth. Everyone longs to be understood, so mirroring creates a triggering effect that tricks the suspect into giving more information. Practice this on your friends, and try not to smile as they keep giving more and more information. It's incredible how well this tactic works, and that people do not recognize it. My friends and I get a kick out of doing this to each other all the time. Usually after five minutes, we end up with big grins on our faces.

When setting up the questions to draw out your benefits, have them ready to be used in conjunction with the mirroring tactic when the customer provides his feedback. They will tell you how and why their needs resonate with what you are selling. Setting this stage will help you in the next step of the sales process. Most people can remember three to five key facts at a time. Make sure you have that many large scale benefits that will help the customer, and questions to draw those needs out.

Take time to figure out the top five benefits of your product offering, and where your competition has flaws, so that you can create questions to ask your potential customer. You'll need those in the future when you make it to selling your organization and product.

Some questions that I like to use to draw out needs are as follows:

1. In your mind, if your organization was running as efficiently as possible, what would that look like?

2. What are the must-have services to help your organization reach that efficiency?

3. What does the perfect supplier look like in your business?

4. How are main decisions made in your organization?

5. What do you see changing in your industry in the next few years?

6. What constitutes a win for you and your organization?

7. What is your organization's story?

SALES PROCESS, STEP 4:

VERIFYING NEEDS

Now that you have successfully navigated the best questions and have pulled needs from the customer, let's move to the next step, which is called "Verifying Needs." Verifying needs is when we sit down with the customer to review some of their pain points, aspirations, and what makes them tick. We are going to pick up on those things through the questions we asked, allowing you to uncover your customer's needs as an opportunity for both of you to work together. At this point, you will need to get a commitment from the customer for exploration. They have given you trust to dive deeper, but now they must be open to hearing feedback as well as options.

Below is a quick reference for the commitment that you will be asking for in step four.

Commitment
Owner-Operator/End User = Exploration
Multiple Decision Makers = Exploration

Keep in mind that you will most likely hit on a pain point or two that will sting for the potential customer when you bring them up. Make sure that you address these in a polite and helpful way so that you do not risk agitating the customer, and be aware of how the customer is responding to you.

I also advise you to review your overall objective at this point. Does the scope of what you set out to do line up with what your customer needs? Your scope of work may very well have changed, and you may need to ask more questions, or re-structure your strategy a bit.

I tend to make highlights of the top three or four major needs. Again, people tend to only remember a maximum of three points during an interaction. I use the main three benefits that my product or company can offer, and then I ask if those points are still things they would love to fix in the future. I also tend to try and focus on this step in the same meeting with the customer in which I have uncovered their needs. This helps people involved feel like I am really understanding them and that I really care, which I do.

I want to help people get to a better place. If you are doing a good job of this and have uncovered some major pain points for your customer, they will nod along in affirmation of what you are stating. Be open to asking them if there is anything that they feel you may have missed. People are happy to give their opinion on something they feel is important. If they do, take note and find a benefit that will answer that need.

At that point, I reaffirm that I want to help them, and if I can't help them, I do not want to waste any of their time as I understand how precious it is. After this, I either move into the next step of the sales process, or gain a commitment for the next appointment to present to them some options that may enable them to reach their goals, eliminating the pain points that were revealed during our conversations. If you are going to be meeting with a group, it is probably best to set up the next meeting to present the best options for them. I also make sure to get everyone's names so that I can do some work gathering intelligence on them prior to that meeting.

You can affirm them that you want to take the time to sit with your team and explore the best options for the potential customer. Keep in mind that you do not want the next meeting to be further out than a week. You want the customer to still be primed and ready to explore what you're going to offer them.

Believe it or not, people forget how important you are when they get back into their daily grind. I also send a follow-up email, phone call, or text message prior to the next meeting so that what we talked about is fresh in their mind. Also, schedule uninterrupted time that allows you access to their undivided attention. Breakfast can be great for this because it is early in the morning and there is less chance that your potential customer has had the time to have a bad day, which can taint your interaction.

Also, a little tip that goes a long way: Don't just show up with doughnuts and coffee. Up your game. If you can't find something that they will like and you need to get doughnuts, though, go big and get special doughnuts, like special pastries, scones, or something better than plain doughnuts. Hopefully you have found out what the customer likes while building rapport. Food is something just about everyone likes to talk about. Find out their favorites!

Keep in mind that if new members of the decision-making team appear this late in the process, highlight what has been shared and open a dialogue so that you understand their needs. You will have to win over these members quickly because they may feel a little slighted that they were not involved in the beginning. They might also be working on a solution with your competitor, so a quick five-minute conversation after the meeting with the new members is not a bad idea so that you can learn about them and their aspirations. You can use mirroring to pull out more information if they trust you enough to tell you what they are thinking. Keep in mind the setting and what colors you are wearing.

After the follow-up meeting, I make sure to have contact information for each person that attended. Sending a simple handwritten note, a small gift, or something else that shows they are valued is a great idea. Keep in mind, you can get thank you cards pretty cheap at the dollar store, and while you are trying to pass the time in your hotel room, bored out of your mind, write them a message and drop it in the mail the next morning.

Now that you have done such a great job understanding the customer's needs and desires, you are going to be able to hit the bullseye when it comes to presenting the benefits of your product. You're going to be able to address pain points in their organization and how your company will be able to alleviate their concerns, as well as how your product is going to serve areas where they need help, and how you are the expert that will help them get to the best place possible. You are on your way to selling your organization, because now your customer is sold on you!

BUYING DECISION #2:

YOUR ORGANIZATION

If you have done well presenting yourself as the authority and as an advocate for the customer, you can move with your customer to the next buying decision, which concerns your organization. The customer may know of your organization, or someone that knows your organization. As you can see, the sales steps and the buying decisions really start to line up at this point. Whereas the first buying decision encompasses a few steps of the sales process, here, the buying decision and the sales step line up.

SALES PROCESS, STEP 5:

SELL YOUR ORGANIZATION

In this step, you are working to sell your organization as one that the customer will be able to unite with to take on the competitive market and gain success and revenue. You will need another commitment from the customer in order to complete this step, and trust is still key for a productive collaboration.

Below is a quick reference for the commitment that you will be asking for in step five of the sales process.

Commitment
Owner-Operator/End User = Trust
Multiple Decision Makers = Collaboration

During this step, you are going to be using some of the questions used in your needs analysis from sales step three to present how your organization can help the customer. The purpose here is to see if your organization can match the customer's needs. Maybe the customers need parts inventory, marketing, or service technician training. *No matter what they need, you want the customer to think of you first for as much as possible.*

The questions that were asked in the "Uncovering Needs" step were geared toward addressing the pain points your customers were feeling from their competition, the landscape of their industry, as well as any details you were able to pull out from them about the organization's internal struggles. Using these will help you show your customer your ability to help them. Your special programs, services, and references that highlight how your organization can meet their needs are things you want to focus on. Reference for the way to create the questions is below. You will again use a few of these to reflect how your organization can help your customer.

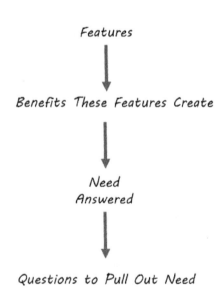

Features

Benefits These Features Create

Need
Answered

Questions to Pull Out Need

Is your organization one that is known for low prices and bad customer service, or one that goes the extra mile to help its customers? An organization constantly investing to make customer's lives better is a great attribute, but may not align with what that customer is looking for. Unfortunately, some customers want the cheapest price and may not care about bad service in the short term, but will usually come around and want value over price later. At that point, you need to decide whether to carry on with them, change their mindset, or thank them for their time and part ways.

If you are a new organization coming to the marketplace, you have a little advantage as no one really knows who your organization is. Trust me, in time, they will find out. When you present your organization's story about how it started and how it has grown, include a significant obstacle that was a setback and how it led to a great success. This will stick in the mind of your customer greatly. You might take a temperature check and even ask the customer what they find most appealing about your organization.

As the customer is analyzing you and your organization to determine how much trust they feel they can give you, providing a reference or two is a great tool to have, especially if the references are from well-known people in the industry. Referrals are still the best sales tool to date, so find out if your organization has some highly trusted referrals. The customer wants to know what your organization stands for, and whether or not it is known for bad business practices. If it is, chances are, you have a huge uphill battle ahead of you.

It is fair to ask the customer what they know about your organization and what they have heard. The customer can then tell you where they think you can help them, and what others are saying. It is good to get rumors flushed out quickly to ease any anxiety. Help the customer to know that you are there to help them, because it's crucial they feel comfortable sharing their viewpoint with you.

I once had a customer that, for whatever reason, I could not get anywhere with during my first couple of years in sales. No matter how much I displayed the value of my product and that I was trustworthy, the customer could not get past the fact that my organization's owner was related to a local family-run business, making the customer feel like we were also aiding his competitor. The two businesses were in the same relative region but, other than that, there was nothing to be worried about. The customer believed that our organization would sell the same product at a family discount to his competitor putting him at a disadvantage no matter what we showed him. I remember having the owner of my organization meet with this customer, but he couldn't get anywhere either. When I sat back and reviewed the buying decisions and sales steps, it was clear that there wasn't any trust established, and I would never have set up that deal without a written agreement between the two companies, equipped with penalties to compensate for the lack of trust.

Hopefully your organization doesn't just stand for making revenue. I am guessing if you look at all the things your organization does, it does not just make, distribute, and sell products. What services does your company offer as well? Does your organization offer specialized marketing that other organizations in your arena are missing? Are there special buying programs that help your customer save more money by lowering their cost? Do you have I.T. that can help integrate software, such as inventory management software?

Keep in mind that selling your organization is not limited to selling products. You might even be a non-profit organization that receives donations to help your cause. Look to find the best qualities of your organization as well as the not-so-good qualities. No organization is perfect, and all have room for improvement, so don't stress. I have worked for many organizations and have yet to find one that is perfect at everything. Heck, I'm not perfect at everything. If you believe your organization is perfect at everything, you may need to do some research and ask your current customer base how they view you. Make sure you understand any market views of you and your organization. Study up and make sure you know the history of where your organization has come from and where it is planning to go.

Like Warren Buffet, I often state an area where my company has fallen short in the past and then how the company grew through adversity to correct itself so that it could be better for their current customers. I quickly follow that up with the largest benefit that meets one of the potential customer's needs. The impact is huge when you come back with a great positive after showing a small negative. People find you more trustworthy when you do that. Think about what one stock of Berkshire Hathaway,

Inc. goes for today. If it works for them, don't you think it will work for you?

This is also the time you need to know your competition and about what they do really well. You need to analyze how you stack up against them and if you can do something better. Chances are, you and your organization can do one or two things that are far better and may help your customer. What is the largest value you can bring to your customer and how can you meet that goal better than anyone else? The focus is on the customer—not you, your organization, or your checkbook. Asking the customer about the competition is not something I recommend doing unless you have built some credibility with them. You do not want the customer thinking about the competition while you are there. Find out the dirt on your own. It's your job. Also, never bad mouth your competition, ever. You may end up working for them some day.

Find out what your customer really values from an organization that it does business with. This will help you really see if your organization can help the customer, or if you should focus your time somewhere else. Trust me when I say that I have spent countless hours on the incorrect customers before I understood this process fully.

Bringing in a couple team members to help the potential customer get familiar with your company can be a helpful way to acclimate the customer to your organization. This way, the potential customer can relate to your organization. Make sure your team is keyed up on the needs of the potential customer so when the conversation goes deeper, your team members can also participate and answer some of the questions. I caution you to not bring in those that have poor bedside manner, though. Make sure that the people representing your organization are those that will be an asset to the discussion. These people do not have to be the top management team, but those that will be engaging on a day-to-day basis with the potential customer teams. Even getting your team to meet their team is helpful.

Make sure that the team is prepped for the meeting, and make sure you know if there are any internal delivery issues that you may not be aware of. I have lost two multi-million dollar deals with a large automotive OEM due to the fact that my counterparts in another region of the world shut down the customer a couple of times that year. It was not until my proposal was taken to what they called a "global sourcing council" that my buyer was notified that my organization was on a "new business hold." The owner of that organization offered to fly to Italy and to pay all debts to resolve the issue, but because the customer was not comfortable with our organization, the competition was then awarded new contracts with them. This was a year's worth of work with multiple groups—engineers, sales, and manufacturing personnel—that spent countless hours designing and developing new technology to support the project. It was all great work, but floundered due to an issue that was not on our radar.

I make sure to ask what other information my customers would like to know about the organization I represent. Asking will likely draw out any potential roadblocks they may be feeling so you can address them. If you are a global organization, make sure that you are communicating with your counterparts so there aren't any surprise issues that arise. As shared above, overlooking this advice has cost me millions and is a lesson that I do not take lightly. If you have done your research and you feel like the customer is comfortable with your company, you can finally move to the next buying decision, which concerns your product.

Consider scheduling a visit to your organization with the customer, a trip to a manufacturing facility to see where product is built, and setting up time to view the product. Taking the customer to a location with other potential customers is a great opportunity for them to see others that are also thinking of becoming a customer. Also, people tend to gravitate toward a decision when others that are like them are also gravitating toward the same decision. This step in the sales process and buying decisions should not take too long, and can usually be tied in with the next step, which is "Sell Your Product."

I was able to leverage this principal when I took four prospective customers on a trip to the manufacturing location of the product I was selling. The manufacturer did a great job welcoming us and planning events for the prospective customers. These customers were able to meet the owner of my organization as well, which helped them gain connection and build relationships with others in their region. During the meeting, I was able to sit them down and ask them what they liked about the manufacturer's facilities and organization. The prospective customers were all happy they'd made the trip out because now they could put faces to the names of the people from the organizations as well as see the hard working people that support the product line. This led to a great momentum for moving them through the sales process and getting them into the next buying decision: the product.

YOUR PRODUCT

We have now made it to the buying decision that most salespeople feel comfortable working through. As the salesperson, you know your product inside and out. You know all the best (and worst) aspects of your product. You have studied your product and the competition to the point that you can probably stand up and talk for hours about how great your product is. And it's great that you know that information, but the customer may not care about each detail like you do, so you need to tailor your presentation to their needs. I will show you how to use and highlight information from earlier in the sales process in this buying decision and the accompanying sales step. For now, you need to make sure that you have the customer's commitment in order to engage further in the selling of your product.

SALES PROCESS, STEP 6:

SELL YOUR PRODUCT

Below is a quick reference for the commitment that you will be asking for in step six of the sales process.

Commitment
Owner-Operator/End User = Need for Change
Multiple Decision Makers = Collaboration

You need the customer's commitment to move forward so that you can help them realize a better outcome for their future. They must be willing and understand that they have a need for change, and groups of decisions makers must be willing to collaborate for a better future outcome. With these agreements, you will be able to move them into this step flawlessly, and I am willing to bet you will sail through this buying decision very quickly.

When I give keynotes on the sales process, this is the step that salespeople are always geared up for. Unfortunately, most salespeople immediately use a shotgun approach, detailing why they have the best product ever. They do not ask questions to understand the customer's needs and, instead, fire off all of the features that their product offers in hopes that something will click with the customer. Meanwhile, the customer is thinking, "This is great, but how does this help me?"

The salesperson often skips the first two buying decisions that the customer needs to make, which is the salesperson and the organization that they represent. If someone jumps right to this step, they are truly devaluing themselves and their organization. At that point, the only differentiator between you and the competition is price, as there is no real value placed on the product or how to answer all of your customer's needs. This is why we focus on asking great questions to understand the needs of our customer and how we can help them in the rapport and needs analysis steps.

My questions are always derived from the customer's needs, and structured so that I can answer the customer with the benefits and features that my product or service offers. I am confident that you know all of the features and some of the benefits, but it is crucial in this buying decision that you are addressing the needs that the customer has to have answered. Thinking about your customer and what they stand to gain is a good start. Knowing the customer's life, family, and aspirations will really help you get to their needs. Make sure you document in your CRM or in the client profile I've provided in the appendix of this book.

This step is similar to the rapport sales step, when you were selling yourself to the customer. Showcasing what your customer can gain and why that helps them achieve something more than a monetary incentive is key. Everyone leans on money being the largest driver for purchasing decisions, but I disagree. I take the conversation off of dollar value so that I can position myself away from the competition. I focus on addressing the needs that the customer has, which are very often driven by emotion. Emotions are a huge deciding factor in decisions. If you can quantify the emotional benefits versus dollar value, this gives you the competitive advantage. Why do infomercials do so well at getting people motivated to buy something late at night? They are experts at making an emotional connection that inspires a desire to need their products. For reference, I have placed the needs bullseye we used in the "Uncovering Needs" step here as a reminder for framing your presentations points.

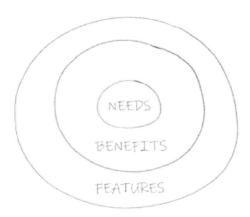

I often refer to when I sold zero turn lawnmowers—the ones that let you step off the back so you didn't topple upside down. I paired the safety benefits of the lawnmower with the question I previously asked to uncover a pain point for the customer. This feature of the lawnmower is an obvious benefit for anyone who cuts lawns in Florida. This made it easy to sell, just by pointing out that it was less likely the company would get sued by the employee's family. Just about every larger lawn maintenance company has been affected by someone getting trapped under their equipment at one time or another. There may not be alligators in other regions of the country, but I can still refer to the safety value of the lawnmower for any client.

As helpful reminders, I have included the graphic for deriving the questions that pull out the needs of the customer in the "Uncovering Needs" sales step.

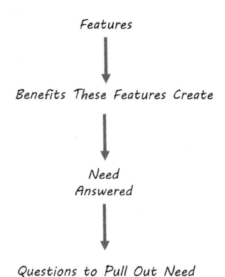

You can use the questions that you previously created in the "Uncovering Needs" sales step to structure your presentation. You've used your product's benefits and features to respond to needs that you asked the customer about. The customer has given you feedback on if your suggestions helped or did not help. You have carefully listened to their replies to your questions, taken notes, and structured your presentation on how your product or service will help them fulfill their needs. You have tied everything back to the customer and their stated needs, and you are going to answer their needs and desires right here in your presentation.

Make sure you are highlighting the top three or four needs of your customer that the benefits of your product or service can answer to make your product or service really shine. Remember that individuals can only really grasp three major items in a discussion. After that, they start to lose focus, and then you also lose effectiveness. Also, make sure you have their undivided attention when you are in this phase of the selling process.

A product demo may also be worthwhile if you have the ability to show the potential customer the benefits of your product in person. Keep in mind that we do not want to perform the product demo until we reach this point. Otherwise, we jump over the other steps and will turn our product into a commodity in the customer's eyes because we have not been able to uncover the value and their needs that will be answered by our product. This is a tactic that cars salesmen have used for years: getting the potential customer into the car for a drive, turning the music up, and getting the customer to a point where they can see themselves owning that car. People do want to have the confidence that what they are purchasing makes them feel good. By all means, provide the demo, and be so familiar with the product that you show that you truly are the expert.

Even if you are an expert on the product, you can have bad days. One summer day in Florida, while training another salesperson on a product, we were cutting on a slope next to a retention pond, and I walked the ledge to make sure it was sturdy, but I missed one little spot. When I ran by the spot, my back wheel broke and dipped into the water. I had to roll up my khakis, like Huck Fin, and push the mower up enough for it to get traction, all the while checking over my shoulder for hungry alligators. I'm sure the customer still has a picture in their showroom of me with mud on my pants and embarrassment on my face. Make sure you do your best to avoid any obstacles that might pop up.

Provide a brief storied history about where the product came from and what has changed about it over the years, as well as why it will provide a great impact on the customer's business. Especially in America, we like to see the good guys win and overcome an obstacle. Everyone likes a success story, even when product developers have overcome some challenge. Telling the story from small beginnings will help you with small businesses because your customer will feel like you really get them. You have been there with this product, and you understand them.

Aligning with the fact that salespeople tend to understand the features and benefits or their product or service so well, I will move off this step more quickly than the previous steps. The potential customer should trust you, be engaged, and close to wanting to make a purchase, so you should not need to spend too much time here. From here, you are ready for the second to last step in the sales process and buying decisions—the step that most people have a hard time with at first: "Ask for the Order."

BUYING YOUR PRICE

Congratulations! You have made it to the most awkward point of the sales process for most salespeople. You are close to the top of the climb and, for some reason, we get to the point where we need to ask for the order and the profuse sweating starts. It's like that time in high school when you were asking a girl out but you were afraid she would say no and laugh in your face. This is the step that you need to be able to ask for the order and not be afraid of what might happen after you ask.

SALES PROCESS, STEP 7:

ASK FOR THE ORDER

Below is a quick reference for the commitment that you will be asking for in step seven of the sales process.

Commitment
Owner-Operator/End User = Time to Buy
Multiple Decision Makers = Time to Buy

During this commitment, you find out how well you have walked through the sales process with the customer. They should be ready to sit down and hear a proposal from you. There should not be any wavering from the customer about this discussion either. They should be eager to sit down and get down to business.

The issue is that most salespeople, myself included, have rejection issues. I had more serious rejection issues when I first got into sales. I would drag the selling process on longer than necessary and not ask for the order. I was worried about rejection. Let's be honest here. No one really enjoys rejection. We all crave acceptance, which is why we always ask others for their opinions in hopes that they agree with us so we can feel validated. I actually had to get to the point where I would have to write down the worst case scenarios if the customer said no. Some of the scenarios that I wrote out included:

The customer will say no and I will not be able to make a sale and lose all confidence in myself.

People might call me a failure because I could not close a sale.

Will I end up in some slump and not recover?

I will not recover and then end up without a job, lose my house, and end up living in a cardboard box under an overpass, being scared of everyone.

These were some of the thoughts that were swirling around in my head. When I put those things in front of me on paper, I realized that, chances were, I would be okay. With that out of the way, I figured if the customer said no, I would just need to move on and revert back to the "Uncovering Needs" step in the process to see where I missed something. There was something that was holding the customer back from saying, "I'm in, let's do this!"

Being totally transparent, it took me about a year of hearing no to finally become desensitized to rejection. I've had customers tell me that it just wasn't a good time for them and to stop by at another date. Keep in mind, those comments came as a result from not following the process. I was only a year in at that point. I've had customers see the value and tell me no because they just couldn't see managing another product set in their stores. I've had customers tell me that they heard my organization was up for sale. These objections wore on me. I also used to get down on myself when I heard the answer no and mope around for a bit, but I came to realize that rejection was an opportunity to move forward, not stop. I had a sales manager that motivated me for a little while by using the phrase: "'No' is the first step to 'Yes.'"

The owner of the company I worked for also used the Navy Seal term: "Fail forward fast." This means that it is okay to fail as long as you moved forward with another strategy after the one that you used did not work. The Navy Seals are not afraid of having a setback. They actually embrace setbacks as part of the learning process to get more efficient. Once I knew it was okay, and if the elite are okay with having setbacks, I kept pressing forward.

When we fear something, we see False Evidence Appearing Real. In all reality, no is just the opportunity to review where you might have had a gap in the process and circle back to find it.

I do caution that this buying decision has to come at the right time in the sales process progression and cannot be started until you have answered the customer's needs. Getting to this buying decision too early will turn your product into a commodity. Without the customer seeing the value, your price becomes negotiable in the customer's eyes. Worse yet, the customer might say that they are not ready to invest that much.

If you have studied your market well enough, you should have an idea of your competition's offering as well as an understanding of the competition's market share. Having this knowledge will allow you to preemptively create your responses to what the customer might question. Some examples that I have heard are:

I have the majority of the market share in my area, so if you have the data of all of the competition's customer base in the area, you can present to the customers that they do not have currently.

I have had customers tell me that they have never seen anyone using the product that I sell in their area, to which I was able to show them the list of landscapers in their area that are using our lawnmowers, line trimmers, parking lot blowers, etc.

One customer stated that the competitor informed him that my organization was up for sale, to which I pointed out that it was a sole proprietorship company with a great deal of liquidity, and the driving force of the company was to take over the entire country before they were finished.

Remember, customers are getting to know you, and some just like to see how much you know about them, the market, and their customers.

That said, when you are prepared to, offer the investment, and then shut up. Yes, you read that correctly. No more communication after you have delivered the proposal. I still remember when my mentor shared with me how to deliver the price. In my first year of sales, I did not understand this, so I asked why. His response: "Because the next person to speak loses." I did not initially understand that. I thought maybe he hadn't correctly conveyed his point. But he helped me to understand that if you immediately say something after offering the investment, you actually undervalue your proposal. You are devaluing yourself when you do so. He followed up with some conviction: "Do you believe in your product and that the investment is correct? If so, why would you want to undercut the value you are providing?"

It is true, and salespeople tend to lose because they HATE silence! Silence is the enemy to a salesperson. Nervousness, fear of losing the sale, and many other factors bring out anxiety in the salesperson. No one really enjoys rejection, so people tend to revert to validating what they are offering, but how do you really know that you are helping the customer without their feedback first?

Salespeople want customers to break into song, sharing how you have fixed their lives. That most likely won't happen. What typically happens is that the customer will respond with a statement about the price that was conveyed. I had one salesperson that had a dry sense of humor respond to a comment questioning the price with, "I thought the price was low, too." He would then push his glasses up the bridge of his nose without a hint of a smile. To that point, the customer would laugh, easing the tension. It was a very creative way to respond to that simple objection. Ultimately, you have to address objections to the investment. Humor is a good way to ease the tension, although not many can successfully pull off that statement with a straight face. He was a very good salesperson; one of the best I have ever seen.

Your customer will either agree to the price, allowing you to move to the final buying decision, or you will find out if there is something that you may not have answered well enough. The customer will usually let you know if there is something holding them back, to which you will have a strategy to overcome any area of tension for them and keep moving forward. I recommend responding to them with more questions. I am trying to find out what needs I have not met that are important to them so that I can answer any questions they may have and get them moving forward. I want to talk in terms of the needs and benefits, rather than simply responding about the price.

You, being the professional salesperson that you are, will also have that extra one or two benefits that answer their needs in your back pocket. Having one or two extra benefits ready will help ease the potential customer into saying yes. Hear them out, listen to their question and see how you can answer it for them, affirming for them that the question is valid. People yearn to be understood. Make sure you help them be understood while conveying how you can still help them with their concern. You should understand all of their needs by now, and have all the benefits ready to use. Below is the flow you have used in order to use your product's benefits that meet those needs not yet addressed.

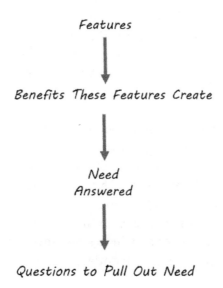

Features

↓

Benefits These Features Create

↓

Need
Answered

↓

Questions to Pull Out Need

Salespeople often move directly into validating the price. I can also tell you that there were multiple times early on when I filled the silence thus eroding my profits, and felt sick to my stomach afterwards. If you validate the price and speak, the customer sees an area of negotiation. If price is the only focus and not their needs that need to be addressed, the product has become a commodity to the customer, and now, the only differentiator is price rather than value. So, please, provide the price and then sit back and wait for the other person to speak. Smile happily, especially if you have worked through the process correctly, making sure you have the decision makers in the room. Not speaking first will increase your sales margins. Keep in mind that the silence can go on for minutes, which can seem like hours at times.

There are some salespeople that discuss the art of effective negotiation, but I believe that if I have to get into a major negotiation, I have not done my job as a salesman. I have not addressed all of the customer's needs, therefore, they are not seeing the true value in the product or service. It is my job to answer all of their needs so that they have no objection to my proposal.

I am not saying that a small "nibble" tactic is not allowed. If the potential customer says that they need something small to make them feel comfortable, I am still okay doing that (i.e. maybe they want delivery in a month because they need to run out their inventory of the old product, or something small that does not radically change everything). Do that while prompting them, "If I give this to you, you agree to sign, correct?" Then be silent again, and let them be the next to speak. You can smile if you'd like to. No need for a poker face or one that looks like you sucked on a sour lemon.

If the potential customer wants to get into a large negotiation about price, major quantity changes, or anything large in scale, you need to go back to the steps and use the extra benefits. Keep in mind that benefits should not have a dollar value, because if someone cannot quantify a dollar value, they cannot negotiate. If the potential customer keeps trying to negotiate, you can use your late night DJ voice, and in a slow, low tone, tell them that you don't negotiate. Hostage negotiators also use this tactic when negotiations are done.

SOME EXAMPLES OF BENEFITS THAT ARE NOT EASILY QUANTIFIED BY CURRENCY:

TIME

People only have 1,440 minutes in a day. No more, no less. You can't multiply them, you cannot subtract them, and you cannot buy more minutes each day. Each day, you are only allotted this time. What business owners understand is that their time is very valuable, even though they cannot always quantify the price of their time.

QUALITY OF LIFE RETURNS

Everyone strives for a better quality of life. People pay for a wider seat on an airplane, some people purchase smaller laptops so they can work more easily while traveling, and some people hire babysitters so they can go out on dates with their spouse. No one really wants to work hard every day without improving their quality of life. There is value in achieving a better quality of life, and some people simply have no price tag on that. Most people cannot quantify what this will do for them.

INCREASED PRODUCTIVITY

Increased productivity is a little easier to quantify by time, but again, most of the time, people cannot quantify a price tag on increased productivity. When entrepreneurs hire assistants to help them free up hours in the back office as well as their schedule, they do not know exactly what the cost factor is. If they stopped to figure that out, they would waste a great deal of time trying to quantify the dollar value.

INCREASED PERFORMANCE SATISFACTION

People want to enhance their company's performance, just like they want increased productivity and time. People want to see growth in performance in the same way an athlete wants to run faster, push more weight, or catch more passes thrown to them, so does an owner want to feel like their company is functioning at a higher level than it was the day before.

EMPLOYEE ENGAGEMENT

Organizations spend exorbitant amounts of money garnering employee engagement at their organizations. I have a good friend, Josh Schneider, who speaks and consults in this area. He is booked a great deal of the time to find ways to get more people engaged at work and working up to their true potential. Organizations are constantly taking surveys from the workforce, having keynote speakers come in, and sending human resource professionals to conferences to become more efficient in their work.

Following the previous steps discussed will keep you out of negotiations. I also recommend practicing with other salespeople. I know salespeople hate pretending and practicing, believing they can do it by winging it, but repetition is key in finding success, even in the sales process, so role play with other salespeople in order to sharpen your skills.

When the customer feels comfortable with the price, you will be able to move to the final buying decision, which I found difficult when starting out.

TIME TO BUY

Here we are, at the final buying decision! This is the time the buyer decides to reward you after all the hard work you have done by buying you, your organization, your product or offering, and your price. Now they are ready to say, "Yes, let's sign that contract and issue you a purchase order!" This is the time you have been dreaming about finally arriving; the time that the customer is going to say yes! You are asking for the customer to commit to doing business with you and to execute the terms of the sale.

Below is a quick reference for the commitment that you will be asking for in step 5 of the buying decisions.

Commitment
Owner-Operator/End User = Execute
Multiple Decision Makers = Execute

At first, this buying decision can be hard for the salesperson, because it requires commitment from the customer, and the salesperson may not be comfortable asking for commitment. The problem for some new salespeople is that this is almost as terrifying of a step as the price buying decision. When I first started out in sales, it was difficult for me to ask this final question at times. I was worried that I would be shot down or laughed out of the customer's office. You laugh, but this did play out the first time I asked for the commitment to buy from the customer. I started sweating, my mouth was dry like a desert, and my heart was beating faster than during a triathlon swim.

One of the first times I asked a customer for the commitment to purchase, I was soaked from sweating through my polo shirt, in February, in Michigan. I think the customer also wanted to make me more nervous as he asked me to wait a few minutes because he had to grab something. My heart was beating, shirt soaked, my vision was narrowing, and I thought I was going to pass out. I did not have a fever if that is what you are thinking. The customer came back and thanked me for waiting, signed the order, and we were able to move on. This turned my anxiety into excitement. I wanted to run out of the store, but I had to hold in my excitement for thirty more minutes. I wonder if the customer knew what he was doing to me, or if he even noticed all of my signs of anxiety.

At this point, if you have followed the buying decisions, answered all of your customer's questions and fulfilled their needs, you will see the reward. Some older sales trainers would say this is where you use the close, hard close, etc. I do not like "closing," because I view this process as a beginning for future business. This is your opportunity to reaffirm the customer of their decision and schedule follow-ups to get them thinking about next steps. A "close" refers to the end of something, and when it comes to sales, which is a relationship, you never want an end. You want the relationship to keep growing and evolving over time. Growing a relationship with your customer will benefit you in the future when they share details with you so you can help fend off the competition. They will also help you by providing you a reference to other prospective customers, take you on fishing trips that you think you are going to die on (true story), among many more benefits. "Closing" is not a phrase I ever want to use with a customer, unless they have shut their doors for good.

I was able to build such a great relationship with one of my best customers in Clearwater, Florida by simply not "closing" or keeping everything focused on business. We built such a close relationship that he took me out fishing in the Gulf of Mexico. He went fishing quite often, and told me all about how well his boat was rigged up for deep water. I decided to take him up on the offer one Saturday morning, and it ended up being an adventure that was worth it. When he showed up with his ¾-ton pickup truck, I looked over his boat, thinking, *What did I get myself into?* In my mind, I envisioned he had one of those huge forty-foot fishing boats, but this one was twenty feet in length and low to the water. Now, I grew up on a twenty-six foot boat in the great lake of Michigan, so I am used to rough water, but this was the Gulf of Mexico. I figured my life insurance policy was up to date and hopped in the boat, and off we went at 5 a.m. from St. Petersburg, Florida, catching our bait on our way out, twenty-six miles offshore. We set up at our fishing spot early in the morning, started catching fish and having a blast.

Around lunchtime, we could see the afternoon storms making their way inland. The sky went from blue with no clouds in sight to black. Lightning struck the water, kicking up waves. My client calmly pulled up our fishing lures and then set out to go around the storm. At this point, my hands were firmly wrapped around the steering column's support cage. We did make it around the storm, getting only a little wet from the rain, only to see an even larger storm coming up right behind us. At that point, we decided to ride the rough waves, chasing one storm to outrun another. We made it back to the docks with my hands still wrapped around the support cage, not wanting to let go, cramped from being in that position the entire ride. I saw Jaws as a child, and I saw some barracudas circling our boat, wondering if I was going to end up in the water that day. Since then, I have not gone back out with that customer, but we've maintained a great relationship anyways, and I am glad to have risked my life going on that fishing trip.

I do want to warn you that, as a sales professional, some large purchasing organizations have been trained by negotiators to make a last minute "nibble" paired with strong negotiations just before they commit to buy. I have seen presentations in purchasing organizations that plan an extra negotiation just before picking a supplier in their sourcing timelines. The purchasing organizations want to make sure they are getting extra credit with the organization in order to claim this extra credit compared to their original proforma in their goals for the year. Purchasing organizations have put a great deal of emphasis on savings targets. I still believe that if negotiations commence, the salesperson has not done their duty finding all of the customer's needs. It is at this point when I like to reveal and fulfill that extra need the customer has addressed earlier—the one I've been keeping in my back pocket for this type of occasion—in case of an emergency.

Also knowing that your walk away price is a good thing. This way, if they offer a nibble for a last minute requirement, you can say, "If I give you this then we need to complete this sale." A nibble is similar to when you are fishing and a fish nibbles at your bait but won't eat the entire lure so you can't catch them. Negotiators use this phrase to get small bits of ground in a negotiation. That is, if the last-minute nibble is above your walk-away from the deal. Make sure you get their signature, though, if you give them this nibble. The time delay it takes to get approval from upper management is draining and shows you are not the person to be discussing things with in the future. Be confident and know your boundaries.

Now you have convinced the potential customer to commit. This is not the time to stop everything and start celebrating with your team back at the office. You still have a few more steps to complete to be a truly successful salesperson by utilizing the sales process. You should obtain the signature, but immediately after the customer signs, you, as the sales professional, need to enter into the eighth step in the sales process, which is to confirm the sale and the next steps to be set up with the customer.

SALES PROCESS, STEP 8:

CONFIRM SALE AND NEXT STEPS

When people make large purchases, their investment is wrapped up in feelings of excitement as they start to purchase items like a car, house, large vacation package, etc. Quickly after the purchase, though, their brain starts evaluating the negative feelings associated with the cost of this large investment. Being obligated to this investment will not enable the person to use their financial resources on other items they may have wanted. When payments are involved and they are calculating the commitment to an item and how long it will be until they can be free of payments, their brain might really start to feel the impact of the purchase. Despair, uneasiness, and queasiness are all feelings people have expressed to me during the purchasing of large investments.

Realtors really do a great job at this step and literally come right out and tell new customers that they will have these feelings, reaffirming them that it is okay, and that they understand. Then the realtor follows up their statement by assuring the client they've made the right decision. They are confirming and reaffirming the customer of their decision to buy. Have you ever had a realtor compliment your decision when you were signing on your home?

People tend to look for others to reaffirm that they've made the correct decision. People will even look to the person nearest to them, asking if this is the right move, even people they do not know. By confirming the sale and reaffirming the decision to purchase, the person starts to feel at ease and can move forward.

To reaffirm and move to the next step, I have always been a proponent of quickly signing the agreement, confirming their decision to purchase, and then I launch into a discussion about the next steps, such as delivery date, a follow-up discussion on another topic, dates to help set up marketing materials, etc. By doing this, you are assisting the customer through the process and helping them move forward. You are validating them and their decision to invest in you and your organization. This makes them feel more comfortable with the investment, and helps them move forward quickly.

Many salespeople obtain the sale and walk away in celebration, thinking they are done with the sales process. Unfortunately, when a salesperson does this, the customer tends to feel buyer's remorse and the excitement is lost. The salesperson has failed to help the customer by not setting up the next steps for the customer.

This is a bad sales philosophy, and it annoys me to no end. By doing so and not helping the customer move forward, the salesperson is only hurting themselves in the long-term. Usually, the salesperson who does not see any reoccurring sales can end up picking up returned goods sold, only to move on to another customer. In the worst cases, these salespeople damage their credibility, which can spread through the industry like wildfire. Trust me when I say that customers talk to one another. They see each other quite often at organization events and trainings for similar products. With the advent of social media, customers can wreck your credibility in a matter of seconds, especially end users that are using your products.

Think back to some of your past sales. Notice when you have confirmed the sale and moved the customer along to the next steps without consciously thinking about it. It is funny that prior to learning these steps, I was winning some sales and missing others, but the sales process provides a structure for success that extends beyond a customer's purchase. After implementing the customer's shipments, celebrate with the customer. Also, you are there to help them, so make it a priority to arrive when the first shipment arrives and help them set up.

When I set up my largest customer in Florida with a truckload of zero turn lawnmowers, which can range from $5,000 to $15,000 for commercial landscapers, I set up a truckload deal worth over $100,000 with this customer for a one-time buy that gave them quite a few incentives, such better margins, great interest-free floorplan financing, and zero shipping charges. This was the first time it had happened with this product in this region. This helped the customer with his company's margins while helping me to sell in a down economy. I was there the day the shipment arrived to help unload as well as spread the news to local landscapers that this dealer was able to make these investments, meaning they were the dealer to be doing business with when the landscapers needed new equipment and service. Again, these were the next steps that helped the customer feel like they made the right decision with this large purchase. This was also not the largest dealer handling this product in the state of Florida either.

If you are selling to end users, make sure you are helping them the first time with their product to make them feel comfortable. Walk them through the product an additional time to make sure they are comfortable with it before they leave you and venture off into the sunset. They will appreciate it greatly. If not, you may become a curse word when they can't figure something out, even if there is a YouTube video for them to reference on how to use the product.

Make sure you are doing your best to help the customer move forward with the product so that they can feel good about the investment they have just made in your product, in you, and in your organization. As salespeople, we are there to serve the customers and help them improve. We are also motivated to keep improving ourselves to be better for our customers on a consistent basis.

CHAPTER 6:
SELF-EVALUATION

You have walked the customer through all of the buying decisions, and have made it to the sales step where you are working to get better. Where I was over a decade ago compared to where I am now in my profession is enormously different. I have had to learn what works and what doesn't work when moving through the sales process. This step in the sales process is probably the most forgotten step, and likely the most important to repetitive success. It's like sharpening your carving knife after a use so that it is still as sharp for the next time. I still, to this day, find areas in which I could do better, and sometimes customers ask me questions that I did not anticipate. These all go into this step for review, so I can make sure to do better in the future.

SALES PROCESS, STEP 9:

ANALYZE TO GET BETTER

Below is a quick reference for the commitment to yourself in step nine of the sales process.

Commitment
You = Get Better

This step analyzes the entire sales process to see where you did well and what you could improve upon. No one ever arrives able to sell anything at any time. Constant growth in the sales profession is needed or you will become obsolete. Trends, generations, and the landscape are constantly changing, and what worked yesterday will not work tomorrow in most cases. Take time to really analyze the sales process and each interaction to see where you can get better. Review your notes from your meetings and reflect on your conversations with your customer to see if there was anything you could have said differently or forgot to say. How can you make it easier for another potential customer to do business with you in the future?

I have a few stories that I share when I am giving keynotes or training that recount situations when I was talking through something to myself only to have the customer walk in and ask if I was on the phone. One of the times, I'd finished getting the signed agreement for the first truck load of lawn equipment—my first $100,000 deal. I was in the truck, talking to myself, thinking about how I got caught up on one specific part of asking for the order because I forgot to answer one of the larger needs the customer had. Another time, I was actually on the phone with my manager, talking about what had transpired during a meeting, and as the customer came up, I quickly ended the call as I did not want to leave him with anything he may have heard out of context. If you are talking to yourself and a customer walks up, always look at them, smile, and make it look like you are hanging up the phone. People tend to get creeped out when they see someone that talks to themselves.

What areas during the process did you get hung up on and what questions did the customer have that seemed to stump you? What tools can you refine so that you are better equipped in future sales calls with other potential customers? Again, no one ever arrives at perfection, so, chances are, there are a few things you can refine. Efficiency and constant improvement is what I pride myself on. I sit down after every deal I complete to see how I can get better. I may take a victory lap for a quick second, but then I review my notes and comments to see where I can improve. I have incorporated this into every aspect of my life.

A FEW QUESTIONS I TEND TO ASK MYSELF:

- Where did I get hung up in the process with the customer?
- Where did the customer not see the value I presented?
- How can I present my offerings better?

- If I did a product demo, what areas did not work as well as I had hoped for so I can practice for future demos?

To say this step is crucial if you want to enhance your craft is an understatement. There is a reason that those who are truly successful are constantly reading three to four books a month. They want to grow and expand their knowledge. I, unfortunately, am such a slow reader that I use audio books mixed in with regular books. Yes, I like regular books, so I can highlight and mark all over pages. That way, when I come back to review something later, it is easier to find, as are the points that I deemed very helpful.

Every athlete that is successful has a coach that pushes them to be better. Find a mentor or coach that can walk you through some of your sales processes and ask questions to help you think. Most people will be able to sit with you and ask you questions that make you think about something you may not have thought of. Having a group of salespeople that you meet with, as in a mastermind group, is also a great idea.

When I became the top salesperson in North America, it took a great deal of focus and work through the sales process. I had spent countless hours in hotels, reviewing where I was at in the process with all of my accounts, what areas I could improve upon, and how to make the next step even better. I was constantly on conference calls with managers and my mentor to make sure that I was thinking through the process well. I would ask them what gaps they could see so that I could enhance my skills. Without this preparation, I do not believe that I could've achieved 50% growth in a down economy.

Without constantly improving my sales skills, I would not have mastered handling collaborative meetings with multiple people from different business units, such as engineering, purchasing, quality assurance, and so on. I would not have been able to win multi-million dollar, multi-year contracts with large multi-billion dollar organizations. I have had to refine my approach many times, and learn how to understand different personalities at great depths in order to not accidentally offend someone. I have had to understand how people learn and how they receive information. When presenting to multiple business groups inside of an organization, one must be able to speak all of their language sets, whether it be technical language for engineers, long term agreements with purchasing organizations, or financial impacts. I have had to refine and better myself every day. I do not see a day when I will ever stop learning new techniques or approaches to presenting.

When I coach people on the sales process, I like to get people out of their regular environment so that we can discuss some of the areas they are working on. I often find that when people are relaxed, it is easier to think creatively. When stress is high, it is hard to think outside of the current struggle. During regular sales calls is not the best time to sit and strategize. After the sales call is a great time for getting to see where the salesperson might have opportunities to improve, and for coaching. Coaches do not try to teach during the game. They save that for the practice field, as they know that the athlete is not as receptive when adrenaline is high.

It's okay to pat yourself on the back for a job well done, but keep moving forward with your growth in sales. If you hit that "Salesman of the Year" this year, you have to get better for next year. Sales is a high demand field, and takes a great deal to keep your craft relevant and effective. Find ways to keep improving. To date, I keep investing in myself to grow and put new tools into my toolbox. Even writing this book has helped me to review the sales process to make me better by thinking about each and every step so much that I am able to put it into words for you, the reader, to understand. To that point, we are just about done, and this last step in the process is of utmost importance.

CHAPTER 7:

BEYOND THE SALE

As you can see on the next page, we have walked all the way through the sales process and have made it to the tenth and final step. You made it! The bad news for most salespeople is that the sales process does not end with signing on the dotted line and never speaking to the customer again. This is where the real hard work starts. This is where all the words about how great your service, organization, and you are live. Unfortunately, most salespeople believe that once the customer signs on the dotted line, that is it. They think it's time to move on to the next conquest.

SALES PROCESS, STEP 10:

THE NEXT 90 DAYS

Below is a quick reference for the last commitment in the sales process.

Commitment
You = To Provide Consistent Value After the Sale

When I started out in sales, I was under that assumption, too. I would make the sale and believe that the internal ordering team would take over and I could move on to more sales activities.

In the beginning of my career, I set up a new product line with my first lawnmower shop in Detroit. The shop was smaller in comparison to some of the other shops in the area. The employees were good and they were generating decent sales with the product lines that they had. They had a market for the stand-on riding lawnmowers because the properties in the area did not have a great deal of room between them, so landscapers were able to get between houses without having to use a push mower or weed trimmers.

After I had worked for over a year convincing the dealer that this product would work well for them, I ran into a problem. I set up the date for them to receive their first shipment, confirmed that they would be well taken care of by the inside staff, and trained their staff on how to sell the product. After that, I was off and working to close some other new accounts. I was pumped and ready to take on the lawnmower world. I thought everything was going to work itself out and that I would be having a conversation with the customer, hearing something like, "This was the best decision we have ever made, to work with you and your team," even a year later.

After a few months, I stopped back in and the original order of lawnmowers was still there, meaning they had not sold any. When I asked how it was going, they simply said, "Good," but when I asked how the sales of the new line of lawnmowers was going, they expressed disappointment. Apparently, the equipment did not ship on time and they did not know how to maneuver the equipment like I was able to, and customers wanted to sit while cutting. My customer's sales team had forgotten some of the benefits of my product, so they couldn't then answer their customer's needs with knowledge. They'd crashed one and needed new parts, and it took them a long time to figure out how to order the parts from my organization as well. This frustrated the customer, and the conversation was not going quite the way I had envisioned it.

Months later, I was back at the dealer, picking up the equipment and having to find a new home for it at another dealer for a discount. I felt like a failure! And I was not looking forward to telling the owner of our organization that I'd lost my first new account. How would you feel if you had to tell your boss that you lost an account, and when probed to understand why, you had to explain it was because you did not follow up and help the customer consistently?

In my studies, I've learned that twenty-four hours after someone learns something, if it is not applied, they forget about fifty percent of the new knowledge. The next day, another fifty percent of that remaining fifty percent, and so on and so forth. Without follow-up and reinforcement, customers will likely forget many of the reasons they said yes to you. These are not good odds when you are hoping they love the product or service, especially if you are hoping they will tell their friends about the product in the future.

I have since made it a matter of discipline to make sure that I become intentional for the next ninety days (or longer if the sale is in the millions) to reinforce everything that I have advertised. I train the operators, sales team, learn more about their customers, find new ways to help the customer use the product efficiently, etc. I have become so intentional that if I have any kind of doubt that I may not have set the customer on the best footing, I keep going back to them to make sure they feel confident, and also to make sure that the product or service feels like second nature to them. Also, when the customer tells me they've "got it," I always respond with, "Great, show me." I want to make sure they are comfortable and not just trying to push me out so they can get on to another product. I am not doing this to make them feel bad, but to equip them to do the best they can.

Do not be afraid to ask the customer to tell you where they are hung up or where they are not seeing the improvements they were expecting. At the bare minimum, it will help you refine your sales process in the future to address such issues. Most of the time, following up like this will enable you to grow your relationship with the customer because you are coming alongside of them on their journey to help them grow, showing them you are not like most of the salespeople that they have dealt with in the past that are now nowhere to be found.

Focus on being intentional with the customer after they have made a purchase, no matter what product or service you offer to them. Follow up, and make sure the product ships on time and that you can be there for set up. Get dirty with them if needed, running wiring for new internet routers, grab a pry bar and open up the crates with them, run them through the new software package, and sit with them and ask more questions about what they may not understand. You may also share a few items from your blooper reels so that they are more comfortable sharing what they do not understand. Be intentional after the sale and help your customer. You never know what will happen. Set up multiple training sessions with the customer to the point that they will be able to sell better than you. Enable them to be successful with intentional effort on your part to help them.

After I became intentional and set up multiple touch points with my customers, I had more customers calling me to meet with them because of the value that I brought not just in selling product, but helping my customers in any area of their business that I could, from knowledge to getting dirty with them to help. People need constant refreshers about their purchases to enable them to be successful using products.

Large organizations hire people known as program or project managers to work on launching programs, large projects, product builds, and so on. The key to these individuals is to work to make the product succeed in launching. A focused follow-up and follow through enables smoother transitions. If large corporations invest in follow-up and individuals to drive successful launches, don't you think it is in your customer's best interest if you follow-up for them?

You may be thinking right now, *This would be great if I were selling to another business, but how will this help me with my end users?* To that point, I offer up the internet and email. There are email software companies that help you construct automated email systems to connect with your customers while you are not working. You can set up quick emails, like top ten uses for your product, for example. Extra support with fifteen-minute webinars that are totally automated to allow customers to watch tips, or for experts using the product or service. You can set up YouTube videos, which has become the second largest search engine at the time of this writing. If you want, you can schedule phone calls as well, or send literature by mail. You can offer product training days called "lunch and learn," where you provide lunch and train their staff.

The key is to spend about ninety days following up in ways so that the customer has the best opportunity to be successful with the product. It also takes about ninety days for people to really get used to a new product or service from regular use. Keeping them moving forward will help you greatly achieve success as well. It makes sense to add as much value as you can in order to give your customer the greatest opportunity to succeed. Wouldn't you want to be remembered for that when your customer thinks about you and your product or service?

Learning sales is more like a marathon and less like a sprint. Sometimes it will be faster to move customers forward quickly, and sometimes it will take more time. Do not cheat the steps. They are proven to work time and time again. They may not seem exciting and have flare like some of the people claiming their elevator speech is all you need, but trust me. The best salespeople have repeat business because they are focused on helping the customers move forward and get to the best position possible. These salespeople serve their customers by helping them.

Do not be fooled by those that say they have the new terminology that will enable you to sell more. The fact is that just like your daily routine, following the process and working through the steps is all you need to see great success. Just like Rome was not built in a day, the same is said for the successful salesperson. No one ever steps in and is the top salesperson. They get knocked down, just like the rest of us, and have to get right back up and move forward, changing their approach for the next time.

Focus on identifying the needs of your customers and how you may be able to help them. There is always something that they can use to enable them to achieve better results. Be intentional in looking around to see how you can assist them to get to those better destinations.

I really study the markets that I enter into and the competitive landscape so that I can refine my approach daily. Focusing on the needs analysis is a huge step in the process that every salesperson needs to focus on in order to get better at finding opportunities with their customers. I suggest focusing most of your time studying the uncovering needs step focused on that aspect at least once a month when starting out in sales, and then once a quarter once you start to sell a great deal more. Always keep refining your approach and learning new things about your product or service as well as about the competition. They are constantly evolving as your organization is evolving.

Help others learn alongside of you and build relationships. Just as iron sharpens iron, two salespeople growing together makes both of them stronger. Be the intentional person that helps them grow as you grow. Use your knowledge to help others around you that want to grow so that they will be able to help others as well. This will, in turn, help you gain influence as well as deepen your skillsets.

Keep in mind that no matter what you do in life, you will be selling, whether you are a salesperson selling products or the CEO that has to cast the vision of where the organization needs to go. You will need to make sure that those following you understand the why and what they need to do to follow you forward. Everyone is a salesperson in my view, and if you want to get better, buy in from those around you, help them follow you into a great adventure. Heck, try it on your kids!

It has been a joy for me to share my knowledge with others, knowing that it may help them grow more proficiently in the sales process. I never thought when I started on my journey that I would love sales as much as I do. I am truly grateful for all of the opportunities that I have been a part of, and for everything that has shaped me into the person I am today. Thank you for taking the time to understand the sales process, and if there is every anything that I can do to help you, feel free to reach out on social media or through my website, www.kevinsidebottom.com, schedule a keynote, or reach out to schedule an appointment so that we can develop a successful strategy for you and your team.

Sincerely,

Kevin H. Sidebottom

ABOUT THE AUTHOR

Kevin Sidebottom has found a way to develop new sales strategies while protecting core processes to win in this ever-changing business economy. The need to be complex and streamlined while winning new customers is more important than ever. Building key relationships that supersede price is a science he understands.

His work with growing firms and mid-market organizations positions him as a go-to resource for getting focused, launching with speed, and building the right sales process for continual growth.

Kevin loves helping organizations solidify the right process — decreasing lost time and capturing opportunities to stay on target.

If you have found the book helpful and would like some assistance, reach out to have Kevin speak to your sales force, coach, or lead your team in a training!

- Web: www.kevinsidebottom.com
- Blog: www.kevinsidebottom.com/blog
- Email: info@kevinsidebottom.com

Owner of Sales And Leadership Enterprises (or SALE for short).

APPENDIX

CLIENT PROFILE

Business Name: _____

Client Name: _____

Client Address: _____

Client Phone: _____

Client Fax: _____

Home Address: _____

City: _____

Stat, Zip: _____

Hm Phone #: _____

Cell Phone #: _____

Email Address: _____

Web Address: _____

Family: _____

Spouse: _____

Children: _____

Hobbies: _____

Why: _____

Goals: _____

Timelines: _____

```
Notes:



```

OTHER RESOURCES TO HELP YOU

How to Win Friends and Influence People by Dale Carnegie
This is a great book that helps you learn how to better create rapport with people by making sure you are focused on them, not on yourself.

Influence by Robert Cialdini
This book explores the brain and how people process psychologically.

Simon Sinek, TED Talk, "How Great Leaders Inspire Action"

ACKNOWLEDGEMENTS

This book has been an incredible journey and one of the most challenging things I have ever set out to accomplish. There have been many people that have influenced me with learning sales as well as crafting this process that I am sharing with you. I have also had a great team of people around me that I am very thankful for that have encouraged me as well as held my feet to the proverbial fire in order to complete this book for you.

Thank you to the business leaders that meet monthly at Truth at Work who have been there for me while I completed each step of creating this book. I am extremely appreciative of this great group of leaders.

Thank you to Amanda Filippelli for walking with me through the editing process and pulling me back from the edge of the cliff during the editing process. You were extremely professional and I look forward to working with you in the future on more projects. Last but never least, my family: Danielle, Connor, and Hope. Thank you for the encouragement and support you provided while I spent hours writing, helping me edit, and choosing graphics for this book.